INSIDE
REAL ESTATE

INSIDE
REAL ESTATE

Buy, Sell and Profit in any Property Market

PETER O'MALLEY

WILEY

First published in 2017 by John Wiley & Sons Australia, Ltd
42 McDougall St, Milton Qld 4064
Office also in Melbourne

Typeset in 11/13.5 pt ITC New Baskerville Std

© Harris Partners 2017

The moral rights of the author have been asserted

National Library of Australia Cataloguing-in-Publication data:

Creator:	O'Malley, Peter, author.
Title:	Inside Real Estate: buy, sell and profit in any property market / Peter O'Malley.
ISBN:	9780730345008 (pbk.) 9780730345022 (ebook)
Notes:	Includes index.
Subjects:	House selling. House buying. Home ownership. Real estate business. Vendors and purchasers.

Cover design by Wiley

Cover image by © Altayb/iStockphoto

Printed in Singapore by C.O.S. Printers Pte Ltd

10 9 8 7 6 5 4 3 2 1

Disclaimer

For William

May you live a long and happy life

CONTENTS

ABOUT THE AUTHOR

Peter O'Malley has sold real estate in Sydney's inner west for nearly two decades. During that time, he pioneered the silent auction as a direct alternative to public auctions, an approach now adopted by many agents around Australia and New Zealand for the benefits it offers home sellers and the fairness to home buyers.

He is the bestselling author of *Real Estate Uncovered*, and is often sought by the media for comment on industry best practice and market conditions in the property market.

ACKNOWLEDGMENTS

To bring a book to completion is a real team effort over a lengthy period of time. While the author may be given credit for the work, the standard of *Inside Real Estate* was unquestionably raised by the many people that kindly offered insight and direction.

To that end, I am so grateful for the efforts of editors Jacqui Macarthur, Jane O'Connor, Jem Bates and Ken DeGaris for their respective advice and guidance at various stages of writing. Thank you.

Ivan Spanicek, Kerry Rowley, Arthur Kolovos, Gary Pittard, Michael Johnston, Patrick Bright and Tim Altass are all successful long term real estate players. Collectively they ensured the material was modern in identifying market trends yet timeless in outlining the principals of success in the property game.

Ethan Szerenga was a constant source of inspiration throughout the writing of the book. I look forward to reading Ethan's book on his chosen field one day.

The team at Harris Partners Real Estate constantly offered real time market feedback to ensure the consumer will learn of the many changes evolving in the marketplace. In the face of constant challenges, I am proud of the commitment that the Harris Partners team displays on a daily basis.

The silent auction process is now more widely accepted and acknowledged than it was when we released *Real Estate Uncovered* in 2013. For the many clients who took a chance and selected us to sell their property by silent auction, I would like to say thank you for your trust. When the wider industry is passionately wedded to the public auction process, believing there is a better way takes faith and courage.

For the many agents that supported *Real Restate Uncovered*, I hope that *Inside Real Estate* meets and exceeds expectations. The greatest asset a real estate agent can have is a knowledgeable client that 'gets it'. Hopefully *Inside Real Estate* assists consumers and agents to separate the spin and find the real substance when transacting. If so, I am certain it will create a more harmonious relationship for both the agent and client.

The entire team at Wiley have been immensely supportive and professional. Their belief in the merits of *Inside Real Estate* is comforting.

Finally, I would like to thank my beautiful wife Clare and our three boys, Henry, Reggie and Billy, for their love and continual support.

INTRODUCTION

In poker there are two types of players: those who know the rules and those who can play the game. In the real estate market there are three kinds of participants: those who know the rules, those who can play the game and those who have no idea what they are doing. No matter which category you fit into, I hope *Inside Real Estate* will guide you toward a successful transaction.

The game is played differently according to market conditions. This is a subtle but vital factor that is often lost in mainstream commentary about the market. In 2013 I wrote *Real Estate Uncovered* to close the gap between consumers' poor experiences with the industry and most agents' objective of delivering a premium service. My goal with this new book is to teach consumers the keys to success in both rising and falling markets.

At the time of writing, the Australian property market is as diverse as the landscape it is built on. Perth is depressed; regional Western Australia is even worse. There are reports of properties in mining towns losing 80 per cent of their value. At the same time the Sydney and Melbourne housing markets are experiencing a boom of historic proportions.

During the mining boom, exactly the opposite occurred. Perth—and to a lesser extent, regional Queensland— flourished, while Sydney and Melbourne struggled against elevated interest rates that were used to contain the thriving national economy. The underlying message here is that both the economic cycle and market conditions play a vital role when transacting real estate. A lot of commentary simply looks to the recent past to predict what will happen in the near future. This is clearly a lazy and ill-advised forecasting model.

Because Brisbane boomed after Sydney and Melbourne in the early 2000s, everyone jumped to the conclusion that history would repeat itself. However, at the time of writing, the Brisbane market, particularly apartments, experienced nominal growth with interest rates at ultra-low levels. The city underperformed against less popular investment markets such as the Gold Coast and Hobart.

In a nutshell, the Hobart and Gold Coast markets have seen vibrant economic growth while Brisbane has struggled to transition away from overdependence on the mining sector. In mid 2016, research house Core Logic reported that one in six apartments were sold at a loss in Brisbane. Depending on your risk profile and purpose for buying, now is either the very best time or absolutely the worst time to buy an apartment in Brisbane.

Perhaps, as you read this book, some or all of these conditions have changed again. I hope you'll find plenty of valuable tips and insights here to help you respond appropriately whatever the environment.

As economies, cities and demographics evolve, so too do the challenges. The first baby boomers turned 70 years old in 2016. The next 10 years will see a massive transition of wealth, much of it in the real estate market. This will come at a time when digital disruption puts consumers in direct contact with one another without the express need for an estate agent.

Cashed-up baby boomers will compete with aspirational home buyers for real estate in desirable locations within our towns and cities. Baby boomers will also sell down their property investment holdings to fund retirement. These demographic and digital disruptions will change the complexion of the property market.

The digital revolution has already changed the nature of the real estate industry. For better or worse, the disruption is likely to continue, and agents will need to reassert their true value to the general public if they are to fend off this threat.

Airbnb has its sights set on real estate agents' rent rolls. Landlords will increasingly opt out of traditional management structures to chase Airbnb-style service and efficiency. Much of the traditional real estate industry survives on its rent rolls. If they don't innovate, some agents face extinction in the face of these changes.

Recently a client who is a savvy businessman mused that he felt like a novice every time he transacted real estate because of the speed of change in the market. The purpose of this book is to bring the consumer seeking insight and knowledge on the industry up to speed *before* they transact.

Consumers will learn for themselves many of the traps and tricks exposed in this book once they have completed their property transaction. Unfortunately, that may well be too late to avoid financial loss and heartache. When it comes to real estate, learning through personal experience is expensive and painful, and the knowledge gained is often largely redundant, given that most people make such transactions infrequently.

I hope *Inside Real Estate* becomes your trump card the next time you play in the property market.

Peter O'Malley
March 2017

PART I
Mastering property

The real estate game

1 Who can you trust?

For many people, stepping into the real estate arena feels like entering the Colosseum with lions on the loose. Is it any wonder? The industry designed to get you to buy or sell your most valuable asset isn't noted for outstanding service.

Attempting to conduct any transaction in the face of contradictory advice and other people's vested interests is certainly daunting. Selling agents, buyers' advocates, a varied array of property commentators, well-meaning family members and 'helpful' friends will all promote their own version of received wisdom about property transactions.

This confusing scenario begs the question, 'Who can you trust in real estate?'

If you trade in real estate regularly, you should have a better idea about how to conduct these transactions. Nothing beats real-world experience. But being in a position to trust your own judgement based on past experiences is an earned luxury.

Experienced consumers enter real estate negotiations with foresight. Inexperienced consumers, who buy and sell perhaps every five or 10 years, are often knowledgeable and wiser only with hindsight. Once a contract of sale to buy or sell is signed, the transaction is complete, and it becomes very difficult to change its terms. This makes getting it right before locking into a contract imperative. Real estate mistakes can be devastatingly costly and take years to recover from. Hence the roar of lions.

This book is designed to be the buyer's and seller's guiding light through the journey. It provides you with both the insight and the foresight of a career real estate agent—the tricks of the trade, so to speak.

It provides an overview of how the industry works and what you need to know *before* heading into the property arena for the first or a subsequent time. Knowledge is power. It can alleviate much of the stress and confusion that so often accompanies what should be an exciting time. And while you can study parts of it in isolation, it would be difficult to find all of the information on your own.

Welcome to the insider's journey, and let's start with the first surprise for many—namely, just how time-consuming buying and selling real estate can be. Where to search, how to search, understanding how market pricing works, the best way to select an agent, getting value for your money, what questions to ask... the list goes on.

It can soon feel like you are holding down a second job. For the time poor, this almost inevitably leads to making decisions on the run and hoping it turns out well. Transacting real estate in this way can be a big mistake. Knowledge, not luck, should always be the main driver.

Buyers and sellers take many different paths when seeking someone to trust in real estate. Some will select an agent who was referred by a friend; others will base their decision on an agent's website; others may conduct an exhaustive interview process. Many still rely on that old 'gut feeling' to decide which agent to work with.

Finding an adviser you trust is vital for a successful property transaction, but undertaking your own research into the industry and its systems should be an automatic part of your due diligence. If the real estate market feels like the Colosseum to you, doing your due diligence is the best way to allay your fears. I hope you will make reading *Inside Real Estate* a part of that process.

Gain market knowledge before acting or transacting.

2 The modern real estate firm

No industry stays static or immune from change. In real estate we have seen the ongoing development of more sophisticated business models and marketing strategies. So what has changed?

Today's agency tends to be larger. Some firms, with supersized sales teams that tout for Vendor Paid Advertising (VPA), inject millions of dollars into marketing their brand and message. It's all about getting as many listings as possible.

Home sellers are usually unaware that the primary objective of many real estate agents when selling this VPA is building the firm's profile, rather than selling your home. As will be made clear throughout this book, expensive newspaper and internet advertisements do very little to improve a vendor's chance of selling. But you pay for it nonetheless.

When a consumer entrusts the sale of their home to a supersized firm, they often take comfort in the notion that they have a large company behind them. Their expectation is that the company is more likely to have superior management and internal processes for managing staff and the sales process.

Many consumers who have experienced problematic sales campaigns are alarmed to discover their salesperson is not representing a large firm, in which management holds the agent's performance to account. Their agent is actually the CEO of a micro-company and pays a percentage of their commission to 'the mother ship'. The management of the apparently large firm with a high-profile brand has little, if any, ability to hold these salespeople to account.

Agencies are structured this way in order to avoid the payroll tax and superannuation payments that would apply to permanent staff. This 'contract' arrangement of outsourcing makes a big difference to their bottom line and adds to the perception of the firm's size. It gives these salespeople autonomy, but leaves them to fund their own running costs. All is not what it seems from the outside.

A practical example of how this structure plays out to the consumer's detriment can be found in the non-sharing of data between salespeople operating within the same firm. You may list your $3 million home with a supersized agency that has sold a number of similar homes in recent times. You are unaware, however, that one particular sales agent at the firm sold those homes and that you have unknowingly listed with one of their colleagues, believing the same service will be provided.

As an uninformed consumer, you have just jumped to the unfortunate conclusion that the salesperson you hired will be contacting everyone on the agency's list, including the underbidders left over from those other $3 million sales. It is reasonable to believe this would provide an important pool of genuine buyers to market your home to.

To your astonishment, however, a month into the campaign it becomes clear that these underbidders have not been contacted. On questioning the agent, you learn that those potential buyers are on their colleague's database and your agent does not have access to them. It's a shock to learn that agents in the same firm will not share their buyer databases with each other.

It then dawns on you that you have listed, not with a super-brand, but with a fledgling 'one-man band' trading under the super-brand's name. This now common business structure means many real estate agents are in fiercer competition with their colleague at the next desk than they are with rival agents down the road.

Given this structure, let's deal with the question of what agents are likely to steer you into when it comes to those ever-present advertising charges and requirements. Charging exorbitant fees for VPA is not just the domain of supersized agencies.

The internet has been the dominant real estate platform for more than a decade, yet millions of property consumers have not yet sold using online methods. It is these consumers who are more likely to ask real estate agents if they should advertise in the newspaper. Why? Because generally they have more understanding of newspaper marketing (even though it is now redundant) than they do of modern online marketing.

Unfortunately, many real estate agents lead clients to believe that spending large sums on online advertising is beneficial and commensurate to the cost of newspaper advertisements. Agents advise sellers to transition to real estate portal advertising—where the agent benefits from rebates and/or brand exposure.

Given the power and reach of Google and other search engines, the sophistication of modern web-based databases and the amount consumers pay agents in sales commissions, inflated website advertising has now become just one of many different marketing tools available to consumers. But you need to assess whether your money is actually helping to sell your home or merely assisting the agent's lead generation and self-promotion.

Pay to advertise your home — don't inadvertently pay to advertise your agent's brand.

3 Will real estate agents have their Uber moment?

Let's face it: fairly or unfairly, many consumers would be happy to see the demise of real estate agencies. And there is no shortage of people trying to make that happen. There are some options available these days. Look at how Uber has decimated the taxi industry on a global scale. As a result, every industry is looking over its shoulder in fear of the one concept or idea that could 'Uber-ise' it. Digital disruption will further impact on the real estate industry in the near future. Whether it is a total game changer that renders the agent's role superfluous remains to be seen.

Respected real estate journalist Robert Harley wrote in December 2015, 'In New York, technology experts agreed the global property industry will soon see a rush of fixed-price, no commission and highly automated peer-to-peer websites.' Harley was reporting on a real estate technology conference where digital disruption was high on the agenda.

The stakes are high, but so are the rewards for those who get it right. In the mid 1990s realestate.com.au did not exist. Today it is a $7 billion company. In recent years, when the

Fairfax results are released to the market, it is Domain, their real estate website, that is revealed to be essentially propping up the parent company. Our attachment to owning property remains as strong as ever, while new platforms to buy and sell it continue to evolve.

Redefining the agent's role

Given the crucial role real estate agents play in generating the revenue for these platforms from consumers, it is likely that media companies will continue to support agents—unless they can devise a way of diverting the agents' commission to themselves, which is entirely plausible.

The internet has made it easier than ever before for buyers and sellers to engage with each other directly. Most attempts to 'Uber-ise' real estate have been made by companies that encourage and coach vendors to go on the market as private sellers, thus avoiding agent's commission. Buy My Place is a good example of a large company in this space. Its slogan of 'No Commission, Lots of Help!' pretty well sums up the offering. Buy My Place has listed on the ASX and it's fair to say it is not going away. Good news for consumers, but maybe not for agents.

Airbnb has taken a huge slice of the hotel market. The company encourages homeowners to lease their dwellings for a short term to travellers at a fraction of the cost of a hotel room.

Airbnb launched an assault on the rental market in May 2016 through its vehicle Hey Tom. Given what Airbnb has done in the hotel sector, its intrusion into the real estate industry cannot be underestimated. Co-founder Tom Baker is reported as stating, 'We're planning to eat into the real estate market. We plan to bridge the gap between the sharing economy and the real estate economy.'

Many of the people featured in video testimonials on the Buy My Place website are classed as 'successful sellers'. This is an interesting designation given that what constitutes a 'successful seller' remains undefined. The company is classing everyone who 'sells' as having made a 'successful sale', in much the same way as agents who spruik the importance of 'clearance rates' without any regard for the quality of the price achieved.

Teena and Andrew Hubbard sold their home using Buy My Place. Interviewed by Su-Lin Tan for the *Australian Financial Review*, they were quoted as saying, 'We have no idea why people would sell with an agent.' The Hubbards have sold twice without using an agent, so their assessment of estate agents will be confronting for an industry that has for so long felt itself to be indispensable.

Real estate agents have had people believe that high clearance rates are the key to a good agent. Now the disrupters threaten to put sellers and buyers in direct contact with each other, allowing sellers to achieve their own high clearance rates without paying an agent's hefty commission.

To avoid being 'Uber-ised', real estate agents will have to focus on getting high prices for their clients, rather than high clearance rates for themselves.

Stock brokerages underwent a similar transformation at the beginning of the internet. The need for a stockbroker to conduct a trade vanished with the emergence of companies such as eTrade. Stockbrokers needed to redefine themselves not as facilitating the trade, but as adding value to it. Their research notes and performance in the market became their 'street cred'. The consumer took the ability to do the trade as a commodity with minimal value.

Twenty years later real estate agents are on the same path.

Real estate is a results-oriented business

In order to make the right decision among these emergent options in the real estate industry, be clear about what the end result should be. People will inevitably be keen to wipe out the expense of an agent's $20000 sales commission. Cutting the agent out for the sake of it might be costly, or it might be the best saving you could make. It is crucial that you judge each offering on its commercial merit. The real estate industry, both in Australia and abroad, has seen off literally hundreds of outsiders who have entered with a low-cost structure, yet there is not one sustainable success story that depended on a low-cost model.

Agents know they ultimately fail or prosper based on results. The same is true of every startup business that enters the industry intent on cutting the agent out of the process.

Real estate firms range from small to very big businesses, but up to 90 per cent of the residential real estate industry could be counted as small business. Given their connections to media-owned websites and newspapers, much of the revenue that runs through these small businesses flows straight to large media companies as advertising fees. At a Melbourne real estate conference in December 2015, it was estimated that $800 million was spent on real estate advertising in Australia each year.

Media companies are unlikely to offer any lasting support to startup businesses that wipe out estate agents unless their revenue stream is maintained. Agents are a media company's best salespeople when it comes to real estate advertising. Startup businesses will therefore probably need to find support and build a strategy outside of media companies.

Many private sales companies have started in Australia, but to date all have failed. Eventually someone will break through and take a sizeable share of the market. The company that does that will need to be addicted to data and cost-effective marketing to enable it. The key for these companies is 'automated connections', with buyers and sellers connected directly through technology. The moment they insert a human to negotiate between seller and buyer, they become no more than a cheap real estate agent.

Can the seller and the buyer arrive at a mutually satisfactory transaction? With the right advice and temperament there is a good chance, although many mistakes will be made and money lost when commercial and savvy negotiators find themselves negotiating directly with non-commercial consumers.

As real estate agents, private sale companies and media conglomerates fight for market share, it will become a battle of data versus advertising, with agent intermediaries looking to justify their existence.

It will resemble a game of scissors-paper-rock.

Agents will be challenged to justify their fees in the face of digital disruption.

4 Insider trading

How does insider trading happen in real estate and why should we be aware of it? Insider trading is strictly defined as the trading of a public company's stock or other securities (such as bonds or stock options) by individuals with access to non-public information.

The definition of 'insider' can be broad and may cover not only industry insiders themselves but also any person related to them, such as brokers, associates and even family members. Anyone who becomes aware of non-public information and trades on that basis may be guilty.

Stock market regulations regarding insider trading are tough, enforceable and detailed. Regulations to curb vested interests in real estate transactions are much weaker, and it's fair to suggest insider trading and versions of it are rife in the market.

By making yourself aware of the many ways in which insider trading can apply to real estate, you have taken the first step towards protecting yourself.

Here are three of the most common scenarios.

Real estate agent (or employee) is the purchaser

Real estate agents need to live somewhere. That's fine. What agents don't need to do (and should not legally be able to do) is purchase a property through their firm while also taking a commission from the vendor. The transaction can be above board, yet too many questions can arise later. If an employee of a real estate agency wishes to purchase a property through their firm, the vendor should not pay any commission and full disclosure to the vendor should be made.

Buying from a client is a messy business.

In the very worst form of insider trading an agent purchases a client's property for their own benefit, without any disclosure to the vendor. This usually occurs when the vendor is unaware of the true market value and/or is otherwise vulnerable. While most of an agent's clients want an above-market price, it is amazing how many have literally no idea of the true value of their asset.

Sadly, it is often the elderly who are the least informed about the market. They also tend to be the most trusting.

If you have an elderly relative or friend trading real estate, volunteer to assist them through the process. It could save them hundreds of thousands of dollars.

The developer's promise

Real estate agents hear the developer's promise almost daily: 'If we buy it from you, you can have the resale.' The developer is offering the agent an unwritten inducement to favour them during discussions. Here are some facts. Every developer makes the promise; some agents fall for it, some don't. The vendor is paying the agent, but the agent is being wooed by the buyer. The best agents won't fall for this empty promise. If you are selling a property that is a development or renovation opportunity, it's prudent to look for any signs that the agent is favouring one buyer over another.

Feel free to ask the agent which buyers/developers they have done business with before. It's crucial to know if the agent is negotiating with someone they have just met, as opposed to a developer who may have bought several sites from them in the past. Ask the agent if they have ever sold a property for the developer who is now trying to buy your property.

Agents are in constant role reversal in their respective markets: the person paying them today is the person they are employed to extract full market value from tomorrow.

In sport, when a team or athlete fails to put in a full effort in order to win, it's called tanking. Watch for any signs that your agent is tanking when negotiating on your behalf.

You can sell ours if we buy this one

It's a fact that most homeowners trade up or down within the same marketplace. Today's buyer is tomorrow's seller. In a competitive market, buyers often attempt to engage agents with the promise of their listing. The best agents are fanatical about separating the two transactions in the interests of their existing client.

Ask the agent if the interested buyer has another property to sell. If so, does your agent expect to be their agent in the future? Direct questions can elicit surprising responses. Just because the agent is likely to gain the buyer's listing, it does not mean that something untoward has occurred, but as a homeowner you are entitled to understand all potential areas where a conflict of interest might arise.

Once you are aware of these, you can make your own assessment. The best agents will declare their previous dealings and relationships upfront so you are aware of all elements and undercurrents at play.

The best agents lead with disclosure. If the purchaser's name on the contract is a company, take a moment to find out who the individuals behind it are by checking the Australian Business Register, ABN Lookup. Once you sign the contract, it's extremely difficult to withdraw.

*   *   *

You need to stay on guard for signs of insider trading in real estate. It's not rampant, but it does happen. To suggest it doesn't is naive in the extreme.

The once 'cleanskin' sport of tennis has recently been undermined by match fixing. If professional tennis is not immune to 'fixing', then high-stakes transactions such as real estate are bound to attract vested interests and questionable practices. By asking the tough questions, and documenting the responses you receive, you will have gone a long way towards protecting yourself against unfair play. Game, set and match to the empowered consumer.

Insider trading in the real estate market is common, yet it often goes undetected.

5 Asking the tough questions

When buying or selling real estate you are entering into a business arrangement. It is therefore imperative to ask the tough questions upfront. Trying to wrestle with the hard stuff only after you are partially or totally committed is unwise and a waste of time.

As a buyer, you should ask the agent upfront to justify their price guide, with comparable recent sales, before investing your time and money in due diligence. If the price guide is $1 million and the recent sales evidence suggests $1.2 million, there is little point in turning up to bid your maximum of $1.05 million on auction day.

As a seller, if you are willing to sign on with a supersized agency, ask the agent how big their database of clients is — not the agency's, theirs. Ask if agents in the firm share contacts and, if not, does your agent have a personal list of suitable leads or will they be relying on expensive advertising?

Then ask the agent why you should have to pay their advertising bill if the auction fails to meet the price they quoted.

Ever since the First Fleet sailed into Botany Bay, real estate agents have been overquoting to vendors. No surprises there. But vendors continue to invest thousands of dollars on the agent's advice in the expectation of receiving a certain price. When that price doesn't eventuate, the vendor is left with no way to hold the agent to account.

Agents who stand behind their promises should be worthy of your trust.

Ask the tough questions upfront before signing any agreements or contracts.

6 Emotion versus logic—understanding fear and loss

Buying or selling residential real estate is likely to be one of the most emotionally charged transactions you will ever enter into. Whether it's our first home, one of several moves on the property ladder or time to downsize, we all want to love where we live. While seasoned investors may take a more hard-headed approach to their purchases, most home buyers are in danger of letting heart rule head. If you are buying or selling while in an emotional state, you can sometimes make poor decisions. Such a situation should be avoided at all costs.

Some of the trigger points for emotional buying are feeling pressured or rushed; the fear that another property in a sought-after location won't come up again in a hurry; concerns about prices moving beyond a budget, or that prices may fall rapidly; and trying to align the timing in a buying and selling scenario.

Whether as a buyer who overpays or as a seller who declines the best offer we are likely to get, we are all susceptible to making regrettable decisions when negotiating price and terms on the family home. Before entering the real estate market, it is important to try to understand the difference between emotion and logic in the decision-making process. Know what the trigger points are. Talk to friends and family about what they may have based buying or selling decisions on. Keep reading this book. And find a trusted adviser in a reputable real estate agency.

Do as much homework as possible before setting out on the buying and selling journey. We all like to draw pragmatic and logical conclusions, but this is less likely to happen if we let our emotions eclipse our logic. Wisdom in hindsight can reveal very costly errors.

Many people suffer buyer's remorse or seller's remorse after the transaction.

Buyer's remorse sees a buyer feeling they either bought the wrong home or paid too much because they were in an emotional state when negotiating the purchase. Once the emotional stress of the immediate situation dies down, they begin to question the logical merits of their purchase. Some who seriously regret the emotional decision they have made carry around buyer's remorse for years after the event.

Seller's remorse sees a seller feeling as though they undersold or should not have sold. They may have made a hasty decision they now regret. Many a vendor has suffered seller's remorse after an auction, recalling how they succumbed to the pressure an agent put on them to lower the reserve price when the auction stalled.

A reluctant vendor who is selling the family home of 40 years needs to accept that a buyer won't compensate them for their happy memories. The buyer is purchasing tangible goods — bricks and mortar, if you like. Sure, the buyer may be in a competitive bidding scenario against other buyers, which pushes the price up, but this is simply the market at work. A buyer will rarely pay more because the owner has emotionally overpriced the property. Interestingly though, some sellers unconsciously overprice their family home as a means of scaring buyers off ('I will only sell if I get this price'), which of course diminishes the chances of a sale.

If the buyer pays that excessive price, the seller wins. If they don't, the seller does not have to sell. This is very common in circumstances where one partner wishes to stay in the home while the other has a strong desire to move.

Many people look back at their actions after they have bought or sold and laugh at their irrationality. It's only through the clear lens of hindsight and logic that they can see how emotion fogged their thinking. The seller realises that the agent was right when he told them the offer was a good one and they should take it. The buyer looks back and understands their low-ball 'take it or leave it' offer was factoring in all sorts of Armageddon scenarios. Because an emotional haze descends on us once we begin a real estate transaction, the clarity of logic is absent. The danger is that you may not be aware of this change.

As noted, our purchasing decisions are influenced by two significant psychological factors—emotion and logic. Emotion and logic manifest themselves in many different ways. When influenced by emotion, you may find yourself overcome with fear, excitement, worry or distrust when deciding whether to finalise a transaction.

When ruled by logic, you may find yourself buried in statistics and surfing the internet late at night to do more research on the subject. You may even be hoping to find some logic to justify an emotional purchase. Real estate investors will often read dozens of reports and reams of statistics hoping to stumble upon the signal that screams 'buy' or 'don't buy'.

Regardless of how aware you are of the emotion versus logic element at play, we all tend to buy emotionally and justify logically. The problem here is that you may find yourself searching for logic that is not there. Or you may spend time trying to find some related logical argument that can be massaged into a justification for the emotional decision made.

Real estate agents are acutely aware of the influence both emotion and logic exert on buyers and sellers.

The presentation of a home is often designed to bring out an emotional reaction in prospective buyers, to inspire them to conclude, 'We love it. We have to have it.' The agent then attempts to build the logical case to confirm the desirability of the home, emphasising how much interest there has been in this particular property.

Some agents will assure the seller determined to secure an above-market price that their ambition is plausible and achievable. 'Just sign here and I will look after things,' urges the confident agent while the hype of positive emotion is being generated. The agent then spends the next five weeks of the campaign producing reports and offers that bring the owner's sale price down from its emotionally exuberant crest to a more logical, market-based level.

The key to rising above the transaction and not being confused by it is to retain a good agent who has your best interests at heart, rather than one who just wants a sale at any price. Also, always ensure that a trusted lawyer reviews any transaction you intend to make *before* you finalise the transaction. Family members are often too emotionally engaged to offer a balanced perspective.

Emotion can, and usually does, cloud decision making when transacting real estate.

7 The winners and losers in all markets

In Australia there is a simplistic thought pattern that rising property markets are good and falling markets are bad.

It is true that historically transaction volumes increase in rising markets and decrease in falling markets. These fluctuations in volumes are sentiment-based as much as they are practical decisions by the respective buyers and sellers. Rising markets feel good and falling markets don't. And they are portrayed as such. The market tends to be seen as 'crashing' as opposed to 'correcting'. But while there may be more winners in a rising market and vice versa, this is not a universal principle.

Once you understand how a rising market can actually work against your best interests and a falling market can be used to advantage, the property market becomes a whole new landscape.

Depending on what your trading objective is, you will be better positioned either to act decisively or to remain patient when you are conscious of exactly who the winners and losers are in all market conditions.

First-home buyers

Rising and fully priced markets benefit those at the top and disadvantage first-time buyers. First-home buyers struggle with the level of entry in booming markets and are best served by seeking to enter the market when real estate is flat. When markets are particularly overheated, many believe—and the hype that surrounds them suggests—that first-home buyers are permanently locked out of the market. This is an overstatement. There is no doubt that boom conditions are difficult for them in the major property markets, but an opportune time usually does come around again.

Indeed, it was first-home buyers who created the post-Global Financial Crisis (GFC) boom as they took advantage of declining prices (and government grants). Those who were brave enough to venture into the market in 2008 are now on the property ladder and climbing.

Upgraders

If you own a property and intend to sell it and buy another in the same market, then you are more likely to sell in a rising market. But you could be better off upgrading in a falling market. For instance, selling a $1 million home with the intention of upgrading to a $2 million one means a 10 per cent rise in the market will provide an extra $100 000 on the sale but require $200 000 more on the purchase. Conversely, a 10 per cent market decline on the same transaction wipes $100 000 off the sale, but a whopping $200 000 off the purchase.

Given that a lot of fees and services, such as stamp duty (and agent's fees) are based on percentages, the lower the price the better when upgrading.

Transitioning into a different market

When selling out of a booming major city market to buy into a sleepy seaside village with flat to declining property prices, you win on both sides of the ledger. It's a case of sell high and buy low. The Perth market, for example, became severely depressed while the Sydney and Melbourne markets were booming. If you sell in Perth and move into Sydney or Melbourne, you will sell low and buy high. As important as it is to sell at the right time, when transitioning into a different market, picking the right time to buy is equally important.

Negatively geared investors

Creating a deliberate weekly loss to gain some tax advantages may seem like a sound and plausible strategy while prices are rising, but when prices are flat or declining the investor loses twice—a weekly loss plus declining asset value. To stay in front on the investment, investors who are negatively geared need a market that rises faster than the accumulated losses through negative gearing. Sharing a profit with the tax office is preferable to keeping a loss to yourself. Many property investors have lost sight of this one. If you get yourself into a position where you are positively geared, the benefit is capital growth that is yours to keep as opposed to compensation for carrying a weekly loss over a number of years.

Investors

It is possible for investors to benefit in both flat and booming markets. The key is to transact accordingly. There are two types of investors—incoming and outgoing. Savvy investors know there is a right time to enter a property market and, equally, an appropriate time to exit.

A crude but timeless real estate cliché runs, 'When interest rates are high it's time to buy and when rates are low it's time to go.' This should not be your sole guide, but it is worth keeping in mind. Sure, every expert says, 'Sell high, buy low,' but how many actually act on this advice? If prices are high in Sydney and low in Perth, for example, how many investors are brave enough to buy in Perth when the market there is depressed? But in 2011–12, when interest rates were much higher and the mining boom was wide open, Perth was fully priced and Sydney was in a severe lull. Sure, hindsight is 20/20, but so is research coupled with long-term planning.

Last-time sellers

If first-home buyers are the losers in a boom, then last-time sellers are the winners, and vice versa. From a demographic perspective, there are now a lot of last-time sellers as baby boomers sell down their assets to fund retirement. Increasingly, this section of the population will sell the family home as they look to unlock equity and move into smaller, more manageable properties in lifestyle locations.

Given the different market cycles outlined earlier, baby boomers in Perth felt hard done by in their crashed market in early 2017. But Sydney's last-time sellers would have felt like they had won lotto, particularly if they were selling up to leave town. Just as first-home buyers would be well advised to hold off on purchasing in such a market, last-time sellers should give considered thought to exiting the market while times are good.

* * *

Knowing what you now know, you may decide to act ahead of time or delay transacting until the market environment suits your agenda. There are winners and losers in all markets. If you plan intelligently and sensibly, you increase the chances of being on the right side of the ledger.

Surprisingly, falling markets can benefit many while rising markets leave some worse off.

<u>8</u> Averages, statistics and transaction costs

When a property sells for $1 million and later resells for $1.5 million, many people jump to the conclusion that the owners made about $500 000 profit. We often see this type of commentary in the property pages of newspapers about the real estate transactions of sports stars, celebrities and socialites. We know there are some expenses in there, but it's still a good earn, right? Well, yes, but it's maybe not as good as we may have been led to believe.

Before passing judgement on whether a transaction was as profitable as it may have seemed, doing some back-of-the-envelope arithmetic can be insightful. The difference between gross and net profit is usually significant in real estate. Transaction costs, for example, are one of those significant costs often overlooked when buying.

There are many factors to consider when working out gross versus net profit. By being aware of all the factors that can dilute profit, you can more easily set your sights on a realistic net profit, rather than a gross profit. Also, because there may be variances in the types of costs that apply to different properties, using a set formula such as 'transaction costs are 8 per cent' does not paint an accurate picture. The following are some of the main costs to consider:

- **Stamp duty** is a *large unavoidable cost* when buying real estate. Each state has a different scale of charges, so ensure you know what amount applies to the price range you are looking at. The percentage payable

increases as the property becomes more expensive.
Given that the average house price in Sydney's inner
west, for example, is over $1 million, most people are
at least 4 per cent behind on the day they settle their
purchase. Land tax may also apply in some cases, so do
your due diligence before buying to avoid a shock or
disappointment.

- **Renovation and improvement costs** is an area that is
not captured by the data in any way. If you overspend
on a renovation, the net profit will be quickly diluted,
even if the transaction looks good on paper. During a
construction boom, building costs will come at a high
price. Disciplined spending and good project planning
is crucial to ensure any renovation will create a true
profit, rather than merely pumping up the price for a
zero net profit. Trying to second-guess what potential
buyers may be impressed by is a fraught business. A
house looking a little tired and in need of some fresh
paint or upgraded doors on the kitchen cabinetry is a
far cry from throwing up an extension or knocking
out walls.

- **Negative gearing**, used as a means of covering the costs
on an investment property, is a fancy term for 'making
a loss'. Even though you share some of the loss with
the government through your tax return, a loss is a
loss. Therefore, before getting too excited about the
house you paid $1 million for and sold for $1.5 million,
consider the amount of money spent propping up
the investment over the years you owned it. Negative
gearing means the accumulated amount spent on the
shortfall between rental income and costs has to be
added to the base price as a holding cost, before you
calculate your profit. Many people who achieve a good
paper trade would be frightened to know what their

true net position was, once they subtracted all the 'prop-up costs' from their gross profit.

- **Rates** can take a multitude of guises. Strata scheme rates, water rates, council rates and special levies on strata buildings all need to be taken into account. Ensure you know what you are up for in regard to these ongoing costs, especially in strata schemes, where sinking funds and any outstanding larger maintenance issues can deliver a nasty financial shock. In the excitement of buying, we can overlook these costs and take the view that we will worry about them later. But if it adds a large ongoing amount to the financial bottom line and the budget was already stretched, then pleasure can quickly turn to pain.

- **Vacancy rates and agent's fees** are applicable costs for investors to consider. One of the realities of owning an investment property is that the bank still wants their mortgage payment, even when it is vacant. You should allow for at least two vacant weeks each year.

- **Landlord's insurance** can be cost effective and good policies are available to cover unexpected vacancies or tenant damage.

- **Selling fees** are what you pay the agent for selling the property. On top of that are the costs of conveyancing—which, in a nutshell, is the process of transferring ownership of a legal title of land from one person, or entity, to another. Conveyancers must be licensed and qualified. (This work is often carried out by solicitors.) They will provide advice and information about a property, prepare the necessary documentation and conduct the settlement process. Let's remember that you also paid the conveyancer on the purchase.

Property can be profitable, but it's crucial that it is not seen as an easy ticket to financial freedom or a 'quick fix'. In recent years, boom conditions saw many investors turn a handsome profit, but the most recent boom was unprecedented and came on the back of record low interest rates. Understand that the property market moves in cycles, so there will be highs, lows and flat periods, depending on how long the property is held.

Investors should take note that net profit needs to be your 'true north' when investing. Too many people make tax deductions their 'true north' when buying an investment property. If you make tax deductions a priority over profit, that's exactly what you will get.

Owner-occupiers will always debate the question, 'Is my home an investment?' Some people comfortably overcapitalise on their primary residence because profit is not their objective. Their family home is for their enjoyment. Your principal place of residence benefits from being free of capital gains tax when sold. Owner-occupiers can also benefit from an asset that appreciates in value while they happily live there, enjoying their home.

By being aware of the costs mentioned here, you can make better decisions along the way that will ensure a good net profit will result when you buy.

Understand the difference between gross and net profit by taking all hidden costs into account.

9 Buying and selling—structuring the move

Buying and selling at the same time is extremely stressful. If you accept this from the outset, it all becomes a little easier. If you carefully plan in advance and understand the right moves to make it work, then it becomes easier again.

Buying or selling in isolation is manageable. However, selling your primary residence and buying the next property at the same time, without proper planning and preparation, can lead to your losing tens of thousands of dollars. There is nothing more frustrating than analysing both transactions and realising the errors you could have avoided.

When it comes to trading real estate, preparation trumps analysis every time.

Understanding the traditional trends in the market can help in anticipating the market. For example, each winter the stock on market tends to be limited. Suddenly in spring there is a surge in new listings. The increase in spring stock can soften prices by a few percentage points. But clearance rates often suffer in spring. Conversely, the clearance rates are often at their highest in February, given the market has been starved of stock over the summer.

Plan of action

Booms understandably create an environment where the preference is to buy and then sell. It will save you time and anxiety, though, if you are fully prepared to go on the market before you buy. This means being ready to put your property on the market the day after you buy, quite literally.

Running through the following quick checklist of items that need to be addressed *before* going on the market will save an enormous amount of time and stress:

- Prepare the house for inspections ('last-minute' jobs can take a month).

- Have a solicitor/conveyancer prepare a contract of sale (this alone can take two weeks).

- Interview and select a real estate agent to handle the sale.

- Get the photos and marketing in place.

- Arrange any necessary finance approvals and a possible bridging loan for the purchase.

Once these tasks are completed, buying a property in advance of selling will be more enjoyable. Not without risk, but at least you will have minimised the chances of things going wrong and saved crucial time in advance. It would not be overstating it to say that these tasks are better completed before you even look at any properties. You are then mentally free to focus fully on finding the right home.

Buy or sell first?

Very few people actually buy and sell on the same day. Trying to engineer this outcome is likely to greatly increase stress levels and decrease the chances of success.

In all probability, you will either buy before selling or sell before buying. Therefore you are going to be either buying under pressure or selling under pressure.

If you do buy first, this then creates a deadline on the sale of your existing home. It is never advisable to sell anything under pressure, particularly a primary asset.

If it happens that you sell first, then consider renting in the interim as an option if you don't find a suitable home. While that may not be your first choice, it is preferable to underselling an existing home or purchasing the wrong one under pressure.

Such pressure can lead to decisions you would not make in the cold light of day. That's why it is crucial to structure the move in a way that minimises the pressure at every turn. The less pressure to buy or sell, the better the decisions you are likely to make.

If you buy first, you are at the mercy of the market from that day until you have sold. Beware of this, because property markets can turn quickly, which is why it's crucial to be ready to go to market the day after you have bought. Many people who have bought in winter when stock is tight have been horrified at the sudden surge in competing listings when spring (and the time to sell) comes around.

While it is unlikely you will buy and sell on the same day, you may still be able to settle both sale and purchase on the same day. That should be your true goal when trading. The key to engineering this outcome is to use delayed settlements to your advantage during negotiations.

Whether you buy or sell first, negotiate a delayed settlement. This way you will have provided ample time to achieve the second half of the move free of stress.

The standard settlement period in New South Wales is 42 days, which is what is specified in most contracts. A delayed settlement might be somewhere between 12 and 16 weeks.

For example, if you bought a property and were able to list your home on the market the very next day, you would have about six to 10 weeks to find a buyer. The reward for being fully prepared in advance is that you have one to three weeks' head start on selling.

In a soft market, you may want (and need) longer than 12 to 16 weeks.

Many people who have bought before selling overlook the fact that their buyer may also need a delayed settlement. Very quickly a chain of transactions can form in which one settlement depends on the next. A solution for many who buy first is to arrange bridging finance until their home sells and settlement has occurred. However, this expense is avoidable if you take the time to structure the move in advance.

Bridging finance is best avoided for two reasons. Firstly, it creates financial pressure on the sale, which adds another layer to the emotional stress. As you attempt to hold out for the right price, money is rolling out the back door in the form of bridging finance. Any money you do pay on this finance essentially comes off your sale price. Secondly, bridging finance decreases your resolve in negotiations. Naturally you want to sell the house and stop the bleed from bridging finance. Suddenly close enough becomes good enough.

Structured right, you can save thousands of dollars when trading your primary residence. And saving that money is just as good as making it.

If you plan to buy and then sell, be ready to list on the market the day you buy.

<u>10</u> Trading beyond the evidence

Buying and selling when the sales evidence supports the asking price is relatively easy. When there is no clear justification in the data for the prices being touted, however, the decision to transact becomes much more difficult.

When the market is rising, buyers will need to pay above the market price. When it is falling, sellers may need to sell below the market price in order to get a sale. But buying or selling real estate at an unjustified price point can be distressing. Emotional responses arise, such as 'the seller is greedy' or 'the buyer is a bargain hunter'.

A decision to overpay in a rising market or take less than expected in a falling market looks good only in hindsight. At the time of the transaction it is awful to feel as though you are overpaying or underselling.

This is what we call *trading beyond the evidence*, and the key to unlocking it is to determine where the market is going, not where it has been. That is easier said than done. For example, at the time of writing this book, the Sydney and Melbourne markets had been rising for more than four years. Many had predicted they would stop and begin falling two years earlier. But that didn't happen and the boom raged on. Given the already low interest rates and the prospect that they might continue, you would have been asking yourself whether a fall in the market was likely. Buyers were placed in a position where they needed to overpay to secure a property.

In a leap of faith, buyers who buy in a boom hope that prices keep rising, or at the very least don't fall. Historically, property markets are more likely to fluctuate than remain stagnant.

This increases your likelihood of ending up in a negotiation in which either you or the other party feel they aren't getting a fair deal. So having a process for determining a fair price is crucial to trading well and not being sorry later.

Quick decisions, made before a clear picture has emerged, can be regrettable. You may find your dream home in the first week of looking, but because you lack supporting evidence the seller appears to want too much. Only in time does the missed opportunity look like it might have been the right opportunity.

It is common knowledge that real estate agents overquote to the seller and underquote to the buyer, so the agent's price can't be relied on. To gain a true perspective of the market price from an independent professional, consider employing a registered valuer, who will provide guidance on a fair market price.

People mistakenly believe the valuer's objective is to advise exactly what a property will sell for on the open market. A property will sell for the highest offer, whatever that may be, at the completion of an emotion-charged negotiation. No one can anticipate exactly what that figure will be. A valuer will determine what most buyers are likely to offer within a reasonable timeframe — that's called *fair market price*. The *best market price* is the highest offer the best buyer is prepared to pay at the time of sale.

When determining fair market price, valuers also consider the broader economic environment. For example, how does an apparent oversupply of apartments and lower interest rates play out in the market in the eastern states at present? Even if you don't employ a valuer on every property you are interested in, it's a good idea to read a valuer's report. They have a systematic and sophisticated approach to assessing real estate.

Equipped with the structure and key indicators contained in a full valuation report, you will have crucial knowledge with which to trade beyond the evidence if and when the occasion arises.

To arrive at a fair market price, determine where the market is going, not where it has been.

11 Valuing real estate agents

At a time when many are predicting that real estate agents will be replaced by technology or a DIY model, it is worth assessing their true value. Some are tempted to ask whether they bring any value at all. It is a fair question.

Most people who have bought or sold recognise that the right agent is an asset, while the wrong one can be a liability. If there is one profession with no shortage of personnel in Australia, it surely has to be real estate. Oversupply in any market suggests downward pressure on price. But is a cheap real estate agent a good one? If advertising really sells, why do you need an agent? And is an agent who is being paid by the seller still a good agent for the buyer? Just how do you put a value on real estate agents?

Given that most people buy and/or sell every five to seven years, it is difficult to rely solely on personal experience. Many buyers and sellers are only in a position to assess an agent's value at the end of the process. Sometimes it's too late to undo the mistakes. The chances of 'going wrong' diminish, however, when you understand the value each agent offers at the start of the process.

Word of mouth is a worthwhile barometer but should not be the sole indicator in and of itself. There are now many websites where consumers can record their experience with estate agents, but be aware that these are often simply referral websites that sell leads to agents.

It is not an exact science, but putting a value on agents is generally best approached in segments. What one person desires most in an agent, the next person may not rate as highly. You decide what ticks the boxes.

Experience

Given the high stakes involved in real estate transactions, it is frightening how easily someone can become an agent. In NSW, a rookie salesperson with absolutely no experience can be selling real estate after completing a five-day course. It is not quite a multiple choice course, but it's not far above it either. An agent with a track record, good or bad, can be assessed and valued accordingly. Although experience is not the only factor when it comes to valuing an agent, it is worth knowing what the agent's track record looks like. While we appreciate that everyone deserves the chance to gain experience in their chosen job, real estate does have a high attrition rate. Check what the qualification requirements are for your state or territory.

Price

Many home sellers, consciously or subconsciously, value an agent more when they quote a higher than expected selling price for the property. Given that the agent is negotiating on the owner's behalf, and not buying the property from the owner, a high-quoting agent is not really a valuable commodity.

To determine their true credibility and value, you need to negotiate the terms of their 'employment'. An agent's agreement to forfeit or reduce their commission if the property sells below their 'quote price' is a very valuable and quantifiable guarantee. Conversely, you could also reward the agent for a higher than expected price. This is not as silly as it sounds. Many vendors are aggrieved that the last $10 000, $50 000 or even $100 000 means a lot more to them than to the agent. If the agent is on a flat commission rate of 2.5 per cent, then that equates to $250 for the agent and $9750 to the vendor on every $10 000. You can easily see why the agent is keen to get the property sold and 'move on' under a flat commission arrangement.

Transaction/clearance rate

In searching for new business, agents' marketing messages commonly contain themes such as 'we sold it' and 'we have a 100 per cent clearance rate'. While there is some value in this from a vendor's perspective, it should not be defined as the primary value offering. High clearance rates benefit agents; high prices benefit sellers. An agent's pay is often more dependent on getting 'the sale' than on attaining the highest possible price for the seller. A fair, incentive-based fee arrangement will ensure an agent is focused on a sale at the best possible price, and not just on a sale.

Database

The best agents are able to produce prospective buyers for your property without the need to advertise. This is not to say you shouldn't advertise. If an agent can't come up with a list of qualified prospective buyers, then don't hire the agent. They are only going to do what you could have done, namely put an ad on the internet and answer the phone when it rings.

After listing/sales service

There isn't anything as persistent and keen as a salesperson in pursuit of the listing. But what happens once you list, and what should happen? Too many people are unaware of exactly what the post-listing situation should look like. Those who have had poor experiences with agents often point to the lack of feedback as a source of frustration. Before employing an agent, get a written outline of the feedback process that will occur once you are on market. This may seem draconian, but once you have signed with the agent it becomes much more difficult to try to build value into their service.

Risk of campaign

Vendor Paid Advertising (VPA) is the trap that most people don't see coming. They naively think they have signed up to an 'aggressive marketing campaign', then realise too late that the agent has benefited through brand exposure at the owner's expense. Furthermore, if the offers come in below expectations, the vendors have to wave goodbye to the VPA they 'invested' in, or sell for less than they originally wanted. Whichever way they turn, it's a lose/lose. There is no way out from pain. Before signing with an agent, ask yourself what is your risk and what is the agent's.

Fee

You are employing an agent to negotiate on your behalf, and doing so with your money. Your home is not a generic commodity; it is a unique offering that has a different value to different buyers at different times. To assess the agent's ability to negotiate with your money, test how they negotiate with their own. Ask them to reduce their commission and see how they handle themselves. The wheels might just come off the whizz-bang agent you were about to hire!

Fiduciary duty

An agent has a duty to act in the legal best interests of their client, usually the seller. This does not mean they should use duplicitous or unfair tactics against buyers. To do so would almost certainly undermine their credibility in the marketplace. The best agents for sellers are those who are straight and fair with buyers too. Telling a buyer they can secure a property for $900 000 when the seller's reserve is $1 million will usually backfire, to everyone's detriment.

Personable

Respecting the agent is more important than making them your new best friend. You are not employing a friend, but a professional to negotiate on your behalf. The best negotiators have a personable and assertive manner. They can disagree with you without being offensive. A big grin and a 'whatever it takes' attitude usually signals a desperate salesperson. The best agents are listeners, not talkers. Big talkers miss small clues that can bring a negotiation together in the seller's favour.

Time

One of the main reasons why people engage an agent is to save time. We live in a time-poor world and not everyone wants to speak with 200 wishy-washy buyers and a lot of 'tyre kickers' to find the serious ones among them. Any agent will tell you that the hours involved are enormous. Salespeople in all fields work with a 'dirt and diamonds' philosophy. This calls for speaking to many to identify the few who are serious. While it's easier than ever before to sell without an agent, do you really want to in practice?

Remember, there is no such thing as a standard agency agreement. Everything is negotiable. Even Real Estate Institute agreements have been written to protect the real estate agents from real estate consumers! Once you have learned the elements that constitute value in a real estate agent, you will be able to negotiate appropriate terms for your property and/or circumstance.

The onus is on real estate agents to deliver value.

PART II
Selling

Prepare to sell

<u>12</u> Avoiding seller's remorse

Buyers who have bought a property often suffer from buyer's remorse. It's commonly felt as a sense of guilt or regret that they bought the wrong home or overpaid.

A lot of people are aware of buyer's remorse, but fewer give consideration to seller's remorse. It is just as prevalent. Given that you only sell a property once, it's understandable if there is considerable anxiety during the sales process.

Seller's remorse is manifested in a sense of regret once a transaction has been made. The sellers may feel they undersold or made the wrong decision in the heat of the moment. Sellers who sell before buying, for safety's sake, can get caught out in a strong market. It is a horrible feeling to sell into a rising market only to see prices on your proposed purchase rising while you are 'out of the market'. This is why many people, wisely or not, choose to buy before selling in a strong market.

Vendors who are not following the market closely may also end up with seller's remorse. They sell for what seems a high price. Only when they enter the market as a buyer do they realise they did not achieve the highest possible price. In early 2016 Sydney's inner west was performing strongly. At the same time, many in the media were talking Sydney house prices down. If a seller took their lead from the media commentary rather than the market conditions at the coalface, they could easily have undersold and deeply regretted doing so.

The greatest protection against seller's remorse is research and forward planning. If you research the target market you intend to buy and/or sell in, you will have an increased understanding of prices. If you do buy before selling, it is crucial to get a delayed settlement on the purchase. This will allow you enough time to run a full and patient campaign to achieve full market value for your existing home.

But, if you are pressured or committed to sell a property in a short timeframe, you may find yourself being crunched by circumstances (or your real estate agent). Anyone who is put in this position in a real estate transaction usually ends up experiencing remorse.

Sure, there will be times when the agent has to provide confronting and unwanted news. As a client of the agent, decide whether you are being given critical market intelligence or if the agent is employing a high-pressure sales tactic.

Be wary of salespeople who don't allow you time to think. Every sales training book ever written has a section on how to overcome 'we want to think about it'. As a lawyer once mused, 'Real estate agents move quickly and lawyers move slowly, and they do so for the same reason. They both know that people change their minds.'

To avoid seller's remorse, ensure any decision to sell is the outcome of a considered position. While a high price seems good today, it won't feel so good tomorrow if you could have achieved an even better price or superior terms.

Be sure you make a considered move rather than a rash one. A quick decision is not often a good decision in real estate.

The greatest protection against seller's remorse is research and planning.

13 How to run a silent auction

The atmosphere of Australia's public auction spectacles in which the dreams of home ownership or property investment are traded is often fraught and frenetic, enjoyed in the main by curious neighbours.

There is an alternative selling method you may feel more comfortable with.

The silent auction.

Just like a public auction, there are times when a silent auction works better than a standard private treaty, and vice versa. The success of this type of auction depends equally on the right agent and the right circumstance. Learning to distinguish each is an important skill.

A public auction sells to the highest bidder above the reserve price. It is common for the highest bidder to win a public auction by merely beating the second highest bid by $1000. The tragedy is that as the buyer didn't need to bid up to their maximum price to win the public auction, the seller often unknowingly forfeits between 5 and 10 per cent from the final selling price. Given there is extra money the purchaser had budgeted to pay that remains in their pocket, the loss remains silent for the seller.

The objective of the silent auction is to elicit each and every buyer's maximum price for the property.

Here are the top elements to consider when deciding if a silent auction is your best option.

Market conditions

In May 2009, after a historically bruising period following the banking crisis, real estate veteran Bill Malouf chastised his colleagues at a national industry conference. Malouf criticised agents who persisted in performing auctions in market conditions that were clearly a 'non-auction environment'. The market was clearly suffering a crisis of confidence, but real estate agents were still listing properties for public auction as the clearance rate floundered below 50 per cent.

Whether it's a public or a silent auction, the market conditions need to be conducive to run a sales campaign that requires multiple bidders. If the conditions are flat, it's advisable to run a normal private treaty campaign rather than a silent auction.

Marketing

The marketing campaign to promote a silent auction is the same as that for a public auction or private treaty. It is important to understand that buyers are interested in your property first, and the process of sale second. Regardless of the sales process you employ, provided your agent runs a competent marketing campaign the same prospective buyers will emerge.

Price guide

A common mistake homeowners make with a private treaty sale is setting an asking price too high for the market. To overprice with the expectation of being knocked down to the market price will cause a property to languish. Conversely, as many home buyers will attest, the reverse may apply at public auctions, where properties are often advertised at 10 to 15 per cent below the vendor's reserve.

The good news is you need only to quote an accurate market price to attract multiple bidders. 'Market price' is different from 'best and highest price'. It is completely legal, fair and reasonable that a homeowner list their property to be sold at the 'best and highest price' on the open market. In doing so, the owner (or agent) is not misleading anyone into bidding on a property they have no chance of winning. Equally, they are making the understandable commercial decision to accept the highest offer.

Deadline

Public auctions put a deadline on the sale from the start. As that deadline looms, the pressure meant to be directed towards buyers begins to mount on the vendors. This is particularly the case if the market is disengaged from the price guide the agent is quoting. Unless forced to do so by a court order or trustee, it is best to avoid putting a public deadline on the silent auction at the beginning of the campaign. Keep the question of a deadline open until you are near certain you have sufficient bidders and buyers.

Setting a deadline in a negotiation is classic brinkmanship. To set out on day one of the campaign with a deadline introduces a high-stakes pressure situation. The Sydney and Melbourne property markets kicked off the first weekend of spring 2016 with clearance rates of 80 per cent and 78 per cent respectively. This is as good as the public auction market gets. But one in five still failed in a most public fashion. In normal market conditions, the fallout rate is even higher. If the owners allowed themselves more time, they might have found a buyer and saved themselves the public exposure of failing to sell in front of their neighbours and prospective buyers.

Lower the barriers to entry

Many buyers refuse to bid at auctions because they have previously lost thousands of dollars on completing their due diligence. To maximise the number of bidders in your silent auction, provide easy access to all relevant information. Have pre-prepared strata reports, building reports and a straightforward contract available. This ensures the buyer can draw on communal due diligence reports at a lower cost.

The agent will garner more respect and trust if they advise any buyers who are highly unlikely to win the silent auction against spending money on due diligence. It is unconscionable that agents often watch buyers spend thousands of dollars on due diligence knowing their budget falls short of what would be required to purchase the property.

Structure

Once the agent has established the field of bidders, it is crucial to ensure all parties are working on the same structure. For this to happen, the agent and vendor must first agree on the bidders' guide, which contains information buyers need to factor into their offer and the practicalities of the process. This will include:

- an undertaking that all offers will be kept strictly confidential and disclosed only to the vendors and agent

- the deadline for final offers to be submitted to the seller's agent or lawyer

- a caution that only offers on signed contracts with deposit will be considered

- the deposit required on exchange of contracts

- the settlement period of the sale

- the price at which offers 'at and above' will be considered

- advice that the vendor and agent reserve the right to sell to the highest offer without first informing the underbidders

- any special conditions.

As the vendor, if you negotiate a compromise with one buyer, ensure the same concession is offered to all bidders. For example, a buyer may ask for five months to settle, so they have more time to pull the necessary funds together. Other buyers may also be prepared to pay a higher price if offered the same concession.

Agents who have been working in sluggish markets are often caught by surprise when a boom rolls in. In 2013 a monster of a housing boom moved through Western Sydney after several tough years for agents and vendors. Agents started selling everything for full price after three days on the market in the belief that they were doing their clients justice. Homes were listed on a Monday and sold by Friday, without a weekend on the market.

In these situations, it is crucial that a structured bidding process is employed. When multiple buyers want the same property, smart agents and owners know it is a tactical error to negotiate exclusively with individual buyers rather than offer open-market bidding terms.

It is important to understand that if the agent distributes the silent auction bidding terms without the consent and full support of the vendor, the process will fall apart. The power in the bidders' guide is that the buyers, the seller, the lawyers and the agent are all acting on the clearly outlined terms and conditions.

Confidential bidding

If there is clear upward pressure on the price from the original advertised price guide, be sure to telegraph this to the market. Do so for two reasons. Firstly, it is the right thing to do for those who are priced out of the running. Secondly, it shows the remaining bidders the property is now in high demand. If you list a property with a price guide at $1 million, but buyers are thinking beyond $1.2 million, it's a missed opportunity to increase market expectations if the price guide isn't increased.

In some states, it would also be illegal for the agent to persist with a price guide of $1 million when the feedback is $1.2 million.

The essence of a silent auction is to keep all specific offers confidential. Just as you wouldn't give another player a peek at your cards in a poker game, don't let buyers see the offers they are competing against.

Understand unique, generic and in demand

Experienced agents know unique properties don't translate into 'abundant demand'. Many a vendor has been inclined to auction their property because they believe its one-of-a-kind status will draw the crowds and the highest price. Don't mistake 'unique' for 'in demand'. Auctions require multiple bidders to fuel the process. Putting a $20 million waterfront property to auction in a recession will almost certainly result in one bidder or none on auction day.

Equally, if you attempt to run a silent auction on a generic two-bedroom apartment when there are 200 similar apartments on the market in the same suburb, you are doomed to fail.

It is crucial to ensure the environment and product are right before running a silent auction.

Emotion

While we have articulated the objective structure of a silent auction, rest assured the event itself can be charged with emotion. Many people feel a public auction is the right selling strategy because of the emotion it generates. Most sellers hope that emotion will fuel bidding if buyers love the property and know it won't be available tomorrow. It is crucial to the success of the silent auction that the buyers are aware the property will be sold and the sale is competitive. That way the same intense buyer emotion present in a public auction will be in play in the silent auction.

Binding contract

A winning bidder must submit their offer on a signed contract. Buyers cannot submit non-binding written offers against contract offers. It is the agent's responsibility to get all interested buyers in a position to sign a contract by the deadline. If you accept a non-binding offer over a signed contract, you are gambling on that buyer, given the underbidders are unlikely to return to the bidding in two or three weeks' time.

Passing in

It is inevitable that some auctions, both silent and public, will fail to meet the owner's reserve price. If a property is passed in at a public auction, this is done in front of a crowd and most likely it will turn up in the Sunday morning auction results published across your city. It will be recorded by data houses such as Core Logic—forever. This becomes powerful information for a buyer and can haunt the seller's campaign post-auction.

If you publicly pass in for a low price, there is no chance of a subsequent high price.

In a silent auction, if the price fails to meet the reserve, there is no public failure for the property, the vendor or the agent. The only people who know what the passed-in price was are the buyers, the owner and the agent. The owner and the agent can continue to sell the property without the stigma of a public failure hovering above the campaign.

A silent auction is the right sales strategy to adopt in a multi-bidder situation, provided the agent and seller are working as a team.

The silent auction is a superior selling process to the public auction.

<u>14</u> Believe me when I say ...

There are certain phrases in the modern lexicon of real estate agents that should put sellers on the alert every time they hear them.

They go something like this:

'If we run the right advertising campaign we could get...'

'We could sell this in two weeks!'

'You'd be crazy not to auction this home!'

Caveat venditor (seller beware) should be the experienced seller's watchword and immediate reaction to these claims.

Many people experience a wide gap between the promises made by salespeople and the actual service provided. If you sign with an agent on the basis of certain claims they make, it's only fair that you are able to hold that agent to account if they fail to deliver.

To ensure you don't fall victim to an over-promising salesperson, make sure you have all verbal promises in writing before signing an agency agreement. If the agent's price quote seems high, simply say, 'That sounds good. Can you guarantee it in writing?'

This is not to be confused with homeowners asking the agents to guarantee an extreme request, such as a sale 30 per cent above market price. No agent can be expected to guarantee a fortunate outcome, whether it's a sale at above market price or a sale in under two weeks. You are simply asking the agent to guarantee unsolicited promises they have made to you. Most people would agree this is fair.

The best agents are more than happy to back up their verbal promises in writing. If an agent won't guarantee the price they quote, ask why not.

One of the most common tricks home sellers fall for concerns the length of the agency agreement. An agent will claim they have 'many buyers who would be interested in a home just like this one'. Yet when the time comes to sign the agency agreement, the agent wants the owner to sign a 90-day exclusive agency agreement. Why 90 days if there are so many buyers ready and waiting in the wings?

To promise a service or result verbally and then back away when asked to commit to it in writing fails the fair dinkum test.

It is very difficult to hold someone to account on a verbal promise, but easy to do so when everything is in writing.

*When interviewing agents, remember that you hold the most power and control **before** you sign an agreement. Use it decisively.*

<u>15</u> Do you have a buyer?

The best agents will always be able to introduce buyers to your property without asking for money. If an agent claims to have a buyer, as most real estate agents will, that should negate the need to spend money upfront on advertising.

This runs contrary to the well-known agency business model in which they profit from two things: they leverage your advertising budget to market their business, not your home, and they use your 'sunk cost' to pressure you to lower your price for a quick sale.

Here's how that model works:

- The agent quotes a high price to the seller, who likes the figure and says, 'Great, how do we go about this?'

- The agent claims this attractive outcome is only possible with a heavy advertising campaign and an auction. At this stage, a set advertising spend for a $1 million house seems like a sound investment.

- When the auction fails to meet the seller's reserve, the seller either accepts less or passes the property in, wasting the $5000 spent on advertising.

Heads the agent wins, tails the client loses.

The agent doesn't want or need your $5000 to find buyers. They want your money to increase your motivation to sell—that is, to meet the mark on auction day. Your $5000 is also a handy advertising investment in promoting their brand.

Make no mistake, whether or not you spend that $5000, buyers will come, ready or not, once your home hits the market. If an agent cannot introduce a buyer without cost or risk to you, the problem is theirs, not yours.

When market conditions are healthy, there are some buyers who will always make themselves known to most of the agents in the area they wish to buy into. They are the 'best buyers', who are keen to pay a good price to secure a property now.

An agent who can introduce buyers without cost or risk to you protects your position in the event that you decide against selling or you don't accept the offers that are submitted.

Exhausting your agent's database before committing to need-less advertising provides the option of spending that money later if you feel that the campaign lacks exposure. Few people need to take this path, though. Once they hit the market, they realise very quickly that the internet does the heavy lifting at a minimal cost—a cost the agent should be able to carry.

If you spend big dollars upfront on advertising, it will probably go towards advertising to a buyer already known to the agent. The best agents have large databases full of current and active buyers. The cost of sending an email to a database of 15 000 buyers is almost nothing.

An agent who confidently claims and can demonstrate they have potential buyers needs to be scrutinised on another level. Can the agent negotiate well? You don't want the best buyer negotiating with the worst agent. In reality, that could end up costing a lot more than a dud advertising campaign.

As a seller, you should only pay for advertising once an agent has delivered the sale at or above the promised price.

If an agent cannot introduce buyers without cost or risk to you, the problem is theirs, not yours.

<u>16</u> The leopard's new spots

Real estate agents love a 'motivated vendor', and vice versa.

You may have heard the saying, 'The best time to sell is when you don't need to.' It's this lack of motivation in the vendor that causes indifference, inadvertently creating an advantage of sorts for themselves over the buyer. The buyer and/or agent needs to pander to the vendor's demands when their motivation to sell is low.

Unmotivated vendors who are ambivalent about selling are a nightmare for many real estate agents. The agent gets paid only if they sell, which creates conflicting motives for the vendor and their agent.

Sometimes, strong market conditions deliver agents easy negotiations, and both vendors and buyers are happy with the result.

In normal trading conditions, real estate agents must often navigate the gap between the vendor's 'sell price' and the buyer's 'buy price'. If the buyer is focused on a fair market price and the vendor wants an above-market price, then the agent will usually work on the party they can exert the most pressure on—the vendor.

When a vendor signs with an agent, they are exclusively signed to that agent's firm for the duration of the agreed listing period. This arrangement provides the real estate agent with a degree of control, particularly if they have a motivated vendor. A buyer is free to wander in and out of as many real estate agents' offices as they choose to during their search for a new home. Therefore, during negotiations, real estate agents have a lot less influence on buyers than they do on sellers.

Two types of motivated vendor

There are two types of motivated vendor. The first is the 'pragmatically motivated' vendor. They may have bought elsewhere or be in control of a deceased estate or be selling a long-held but profitable investment. These vendors accept the best market price and sell. They are motivated enough that the agent does not have a particularly difficult time 'controlling' the vendor. This allows the agent to focus on obtaining each potential buyer's best price, confident that the vendor will accept the highest offer.

The second type of vendor is the 'artificially motivated' one. They are only motivated to sell if the price is right. Strangely enough, though, they find themselves moving the tenants out of their investment property, committing thousands of dollars to hiring furniture and spending several thousand more on internet ads.

Motivation can lead to over-expenditure

'Bigger photos equal more buyers,' agents assure vendors. 'Make your property stand out in the crowd. You cannot sell a secret.' The tired clichés agents once used to sell needless newspaper ads are now being used to sell unnecessarily expensive internet campaigns.

'If you are not on page one you have erected a billboard in the forest,' screams the real estate trainer hired to increase the amount of Vendor Paid Advertising (VPA) sold by agents.

Negotiators call it the *sunk cost syndrome*. If you can get someone to invest in an outcome upfront—emotionally or financially—then they are substantially more motivated to want a return on their investment.

The sunk cost syndrome allows agents to sell unmotivated vendors a poison pill in the form of increased exposure. Once the vendor swallows that pill, they have unwittingly increased their motivation to sell tenfold. Agents therefore now love expensive internet ads for exactly the same reason they loved expensive newspaper ads.

The real estate industry still proudly spruiks the idea that campaigns using print marketing have higher clearance rates than those that don't. That's a weird conclusion to draw when you consider home buyers rarely look at print ads now.

What the industry declines to admit is that vendors cajoled into spending money on a print campaign have needlessly spent good money on bad advertising. While their agent has caused them to become more motivated to sell, they have also encouraged them to pay for advertising in a medium that buyers deserted en masse some years ago.

To determine whether expensive internet ads work, let's look at them from the buyer's perspective.

As a buyer, would you accept or reject a property based on the size of the respective ads or photographs? Would you enjoy living in a home featured on page one more than those listed on page three? Are you more or less likely to inspect a home because the internet site allows you to go on a video tour? If, like most buyers, you are less likely to inspect the home because you have now seen inside, then why would you pay to run a video tour advertisement in the first place?

A few probing questions uncover some surprising answers!

Agents buy subscription packages from advertisers, and this forces them to run expensive web campaigns. The rules are simple. Either the consumer or the agent must pay upfront for these ads, regardless of the outcome of the sales campaign. It is easy to see, then, where an agent's passion for selling vendors this type of expensive internet advertising is coming from.

Currently in Australian real estate circles the greatest fear is of all-out digital disruption. Industry forums are full of agents who feel their Uber moment is imminent. And it may well be true, if they continue to charge home vendors thousands of dollars for expensive, unnecessary internet campaigns when cost-effective internet campaigns work just as well, if not better.

It is important to note that stock brokers love big real estate websites. They are deemed to be 'high-margin businesses' — that is, they have low costs and high incomes. Their cost base has barely risen as their volume of business and income has exploded in recent years. Rightmove, the premier real estate site in the UK, has seen its share price explode since it went public. The company's de facto salespeople are real estate agents in the field talking to homeowners about the benefits of advertising on the site.

Zillow, the number one real estate portal in the US, is attempting to replicate elements of the Australian model of VPA, among other strategies. Many of the major shareholders in Zillow have been Australian businessmen looking for the next realestate.com.au. They appreciate the profitability of a dominant real estate portal, where real estate agents act as unofficial advertising salespeople for the site.

The leopard may have changed its spots, from newspaper ads to internet ads, but vendors should beware — it is still a leopard.

<u>17</u> Mystery shop the agent

You are most likely to select your selling agent from a sales proposal process or an interview. However you decide, bear in mind that neither option actually shows the agent in action. Agents work from fully rehearsed scripts designed to ensure a slick presentation and a 'decisive close'. Given an agent is being employed to market, sell and negotiate the sale, it is well worth viewing them in the field.

To gain a clearer perspective, mystery shop them as a buyer. By asking a few key questions you will rapidly gain an insight into whether the agent is the right one for you. Questions such as 'Why hasn't the property sold yet?' or 'Do you have sales evidence to justify the price guide?' can produce surprising answers.

Every agent will find it easy to hold the line with a new listing that has a lot of interest in it. A better insight into their abilities can be gained by mystery shopping them on one of their failed auctions or struggling campaigns. Look for clues to whether the agent is protecting their client's interests or breaching confidence.

The best agents are those who protect their clients, even when the campaign is not going to script. A dangerous agent for the vendor is one who becomes desperate when the campaign does not go as expected.

All agents look good when there are three buyers trying to buy one house. How does the same agent perform when the property has failed at auction, the advertising money has been spent (wasted) and the crowds have stopped turning up to the open inspections?

Here's what to look for when you mystery shop an agent:

- **Availability.** You want an agent who is available. Do they respond to messages? It is a common phenomenon in real estate that the stronger the market, the worse the service buyers receive. Essentially, in a boom, service to buyers goes down as agents' advertising for home buyers goes up!

- **Follow-up and follow-through.** Did you get the information requested? After the inspection, was there a follow-up contact for feedback and an invitation for a second inspection? Were you informed of similar properties being listed the week after that inspection? Is a senior or listing agent handling your enquiry or was it delegated to the office junior who started in real estate last week?

- **Enthusiasm**. Was the agent enthusiastic about the property and you as a buyer?

- **Knowledge**. The best agents have a thorough knowledge of the property and the local area. If there is a question the agent can't answer on the spot, they should chase the answer and respond as soon as possible.

- **Assertiveness.** Look for agents who are pleasant but assertive. When asking probing test questions, they confidently and assertively protect their clients. A pleasant eager-to-pleaser won't help when the negotiating gets down to the pointy end of proceedings.

Here's what you don't want to see when you mystery shop an agent:

- **Disclosure of personal details.** If you leave an inspection feeling as though you know the owner's life story because the agent divulged all, that's not a good thing. It is actually a terrible betrayal. If you are told the owners are selling because 'a job loss caused financial difficulties, which led to stress in the marriage, which saw one of the owners begin an affair, which was the cause of the divorce', do not hire that agent!

- **Short temper, rudeness or unavailability.** The best salespeople know the next enquiry could be the best buyer. Conversely, if the agent is abrasive and pre-judges buyers, they are likely to turn buyers off the home.

- **Other buyers' offers.** Some agents will freely disclose offers made by other buyers. This breeds instant mistrust in buyers. If offers are disclosed, expect yours to be as well. An agent who does this during a sales campaign is effectively running a 'Dutch auction'. The property will be 'sold to the buyer who offers the best price' is a simple and assertive response to this.

There are many elements to choosing the right agent. The most dangerous (and lazy) selection method is to request three agents inspect your property and send a written sales proposal. Given $50 000 or $100 000 can be easily gained or lost during the campaign, it is worth finding the right agent.

Mystery shopping is a proven method of helping to select a competent negotiator.

<u>18</u> Expensive web advertising drives off-market transactions

Real estate agents across the country are increasingly moving towards off-market transactions. An off-market transaction is defined as one where the agent markets the property only to their database and known buyers, rather than listing on prominent media websites.

Given the sophistication of industry customer relationship managers (CRMs), it is plausible that a real estate agent can expose a property to the vast majority of active buyers in the market. But these CRMs have been around for quite some time. While they facilitate the effectiveness of off-market sales, they are not the cause of the recent spike in transactions.

Off-market transactions have spiked because agents and consumers are looking to avoid the high cost of real estate websites. Startup businesses that began in a garage less than 20 years ago are now billion-dollar companies off the back of real estate advertising. The price that agents and home sellers have been asked to pay for a web listing has increased nearly every year for the past two decades. Agents happily went along with the price increases because they simply passed them on to the vendor. Now the vendor does not want to pay!

We are at a stage where the market is beginning to reach a price-resistance point. Private sale companies promising to save the consumer commission flank agents to the left, while excessive advertising fees flank them to the right. The real estate agent is being squeezed by a cheaper competitor on one side, and an unjustified expense on the other. Agents need to innovate to survive.

Agents who have signed lengthy contracts committing to present every listing as an upgraded prestige or premiere listing are feeling the price pressure the most. Consumers inherently know that you don't need to spend $5000 or $10 000 on web advertising to find buyers. Particularly in a boom.

One example of how this can work in boom conditions involves a vendor named Keith, who decided to sell his Rodd Point home of 30 years. He felt it was worth between $1.5 and $1.6 million. Keith's agent, Charles, offered to show through some buyers from his database to ensure that Keith's price expectations could be met. After one of the inspections one buyer knocked on Keith's door and offered him $1.7 million. Keith was delighted, to say the least. Fortunately for him, he did not sign a contract with the buyer. Charles was more circumspect and encouraged Keith to list on the open market and maximise the pool of potential buyers. 'Why sell within a select group of buyers when we can open the sale to the highest offer?' he reasoned.

Keith's sale turned into an ultra-competitive silent auction. He received three offers above $1.7 million and eventually sold for $1.875 million, eight days after he nearly sold for $1.7 million off-market.

Most of the money spent on web promotion is about building the agent's profile or brand. There is absolutely no research to suggest that home buyers respond more favourably to a property because it is or isn't the subject of a large, expensive advertisement.

People buy homes, not real estate advertisements. Sellers are well advised to keep this in mind. If an agent asks you to fork out huge amounts of money on an expensive web campaign, tell them your aim is to sell your home, not to buy advertising. If the agent passionately believes in the product, they can pay.

It is this pushback from consumers that is inadvertently driving off-market transactions. The consumer refuses to pay for expensive web ads, and increasingly agents do too. Off-market transactions are becoming the happy medium between agent and consumer.

It is understandable that consumers will need to weigh up the potential benefit of listing on the open market versus trading off-market. Agents are increasingly building real and perceived benefits into their pitch when it comes to off-market selling. The consumer needs to ascertain whether the agent is simply looking to avoid the excessive advertising costs they have committed to.

Just because you can sell off-market does not mean you should. Agents are increasingly selling properties off-market to avoid advertising fees.

<u>19</u> Are you choosing a valuer or a negotiator?

The simple task of selecting an agent to sell your home can become problematic very quickly. Many agents will pitch for your business, and choosing the right one won't necessarily be a straightforward decision. It becomes all the more challenging if you don't know how to identify a good agent from one who over-promises and under-delivers.

When interviewing real estate agents, sellers will often focus on two selection criteria: the price the agent feels the property is worth and the agent's selling fee. This is flawed reasoning and often leads to the wrong agent being hired. Remember: an agent is not a valuer. All agents you interview will have an opinion on the likely value of your property, and that's all it is—an opinion of value.

Ultimately, a real estate agent's job is to maximise the sale price on behalf of the seller in a timely fashion. If all you want is a price on your home, call a valuer, not a real estate agent. When interviewing and selecting an agent, therefore, you need to examine the entire proposed selling strategy—the agent's suggested marketing and negotiation process. The best agent is the one with the best selling strategy, not the highest price quote.

If the owner signs up with the most price-optimistic agent and commits to a $10 000 advertising campaign over 90 days, hoping the agent is telling the truth around price, it will most likely end in tears.

Often people will sign with the agent using a selling strategy they don't like, such as auction, purely because they like the price the agent quoted. This seems sensible enough. However, if you interview real estate agents and don't bring the selection criteria back to the proposed selling strategy, you will be plunging into a world of confusion.

If the agent has a thorough understanding of property prices in the respective marketplace, that's a sufficient starting point to then begin examining the agent's selling strategy.

Any prices quoted by agents should be backed by sales evidence. A proposed selling price without supporting sales evidence should be taken with a pinch of salt. It's easy for an agent to quote a high price to a property seller, but it takes genuine knowledge and skill to defend the price with sales evidence to a buyer when the home hits the market.

Finally, never tell the agent what you feel the home is worth. We are all susceptible to believing what we want to hear. Keep the focus on how the agent will negotiate the highest possible price from every buyer for you.

In terms of commission, fees and advertising costs, the cheapest agent is the one who leaves the most money in your pocket after the sale has occurred. An agent who cuts their commission by 1 per cent to get the listing is one who more than likely cuts price, rather than building value. Do you want an agent who cuts price to get a deal done or one who builds value into the offering?

It may feel good to get the agent's fees down at the time of listing, but it won't feel so good if a buyer is out-negotiating your incompetent agent a few weeks later.

When it comes to paying real estate agents, cheap is rarely good and good is rarely cheap. The best agents maximise price in a strong market and protect price in a falling market.

Agents are not valuers. You are looking to employ professional negotiators with strong market knowledge and carefully nurtured databases of buyers.

<u>20</u> Seven questions to ask when selling

Taking the time to understand and ask seven questions before you sign with any agent can go a long way to ensuring you make the right choice.

1. What evidence did you rely on when valuing our property?

We are all susceptible to believing what we want to hear. If an agent quotes a high price for your property, it's natural to want to believe them. However, an agent who cannot justify their price to you as the owner will have an even harder time convincing a buyer.

2. If the property sells below your quoted price, do we still have to pay full commission?

When you sign an agency agreement to sell, the agent must provide a written assessment of value. You, as the seller, enter into the agreement based in part on the agent's written assessment. If the agent fails to achieve their promised assessment of value, you should have an ability to penalise the agent for getting it wrong.

By being firm on this point when interviewing agents, you will flush out what the agent really thinks your home is worth.

3. How do you have an auction with one buyer?

It is staggering how many homeowners list for auction without knowing the answer to this question. Clearly, auctions rely on competition — that is, multiple bidders.

Unique homes often require unique buyers. In soft markets, you can be fortunate to have even one buyer. What happens if only one buyer attends the auction?

What if two buyers attend the auction, where one absolutely loves the home and the other is a bargain hunter? The bargain hunter sets the price at which the emotional buyer becomes the highest bidder.

Resist signing with an agent until they offer a plausible explanation on how they handle a situation where they have only one buyer at the auction.

4. What strategy will you employ to get the highest price for our property?

Agents love to talk about 'clearance rates' when selling and marketing their firm. As a home seller, you want a high price, not to be part of an agent's clearance results. Focus on the agent with the best strategy for achieving the highest price, not for clearing housing stock quickly.

The time to ask tough questions about the agent's strategy is before you employ them. The agent is less able to wave you away if you grill them prior to listing. After all, you will be paying a lot of money for the agent's service, so it's best everyone is on the same page before you begin.

5. If you already have buyers, why do we need to pay advertising upfront to reach those same buyers?

It's the greatest paradox in the market. The agent claims to have readily available buyers, and then asks for advertising money to find buyers. Why?

6. Which agent will attend the inspections with buyers?

Many lead agents will list the property and then palm off the selling of the property to a junior or assistant. Get it in writing that the agent you list with will be the agent handling inspections and negotiations. You don't want the sale of your home to be treated as a training exercise. In fairness, it's not that junior salespeople won't be involved in the process, but you need to be completely clear about the experience of the agent who will be leading negotiations in the campaign.

7. Can we have the names and contact numbers of 10 previous clients?

Real estate agents sell houses to buyers and services to sellers. The house is tangible, but the service is intangible. Judging the value of any service in advance of actually receiving the service is difficult. Speak to the agent's recent clients to understand whether the promises match the delivery.

Ask the hard questions first, **before you sign.** *Saving the tough questions until later, when the campaign is in trouble, is too late.*

<u>21</u> Are valuers conservative?

Whenever the topic of valuers arises, the claim that they are too conservative always pops up, almost on autocue. The notion that they are deliberately conservative is a long-held belief in the community. It's worth assessing the validity of this claim.

There are numerous factors to consider when it comes to independent valuations that can help you appreciate a valuation report for what it is.

As vendor, your goal is simply to sell your property to the buyer who is prepared to pay the highest price in the market. Homeowners and agents will often assess a property based on what they think a buyer would pay. They subconsciously disregard the price cut-off point at which many buyers would be willing to buy the property. Their focus, correctly, is on the highest possible price the best buyer might pay. After all, that's the goal!

Valuers, however, have a different goal. They need to advise in writing—for which they are legally liable—the price at which the property will definitely sell at the time they write their report. They don't have the luxury of speculating on whether one buyer will fall in love with the property and pay a premium price to purchase it. Market price is the price point at which there is a market—that is, more than one solitary buyer.

Valuers will often talk with agents before signing off on a property's value. They do so in order to find out about recent sales. They want details of any recent sales that may have impacted the market so they can include them in their report.

Yet very few agents will talk with a valuer before signing off on a market appraisal. The agent may look at a few comparable recent sales, assess general market conditions and arrive at a range that spans from pessimistic to optimistic. The agent often factors in how buyer emotion may or may not impact on selling the property. Valuers do not.

A curbside bank valuation or loan approval based on an internet ad must not be confused with an independent valuation. If the valuer has not inspected the property and written a report based on their findings, it's not a proper valuation.

Valuers can look conservative in a rising market too, because they are hesitant to accept new pricing platforms until an undeniable trend has been well established.

Rarely will a property sell for significantly less than an independent valuation indicates it is worth: most often it will sell within a few percentage points.

Valuers are trained to be accurate, not conservative.

<u>22</u> Overquoting

Real estate is an extremely competitive game. Exclusive listing rights are the quarry and inflating the suggested selling price is a long-adopted tactic of many agents in the hunt for stock.

Sellers need to be wary of the likelihood that agents are overquoting. Selecting your selling agent on solely the price they quote is unwise. If you openly select on price you inadvertently create a bidding war among the agents. Some agents will become vague and speculative in their assessment of value.

Watch for bold statements and loose promises such as 'I think we can get up to...' or 'At an auction, who knows, the price could even reach...' and the old chestnut 'We have a cashed-up buyer that only wants to deal with our office, but they will pay above market price for your home.'

These assertions are designed to create a feel-good atmosphere at the time of listing. But once the home hits the market, if the promises can't be executed by the agent, the campaign can quickly deteriorate.

The two great dangers in overquoting

Many home sellers learn about the downside of this practice only when it's too late.

The first danger is the scenario in which the seller purchases another property before they have sold their existing dwelling. They buy on the basis of the inflated price guide on the existing home—a price, as they are soon to realise, that is unattainable on the open market. This scenario is common. Those who have been through the process are often left financially compromised and emotionally drained. To buy for $2 million, thinking you can sell for $1 million (or 'more at auction'), but only achieving $880 000, creates a devastating black hole in the budget.

There are boom-time examples of people selling for $500 000 less than the agent quoted. They sold for dramatically less because they had to, having committed elsewhere.

As an initial safety measure, when buying a house from an agent before you have sold, ensure you get multiple appraisals from agents and/or an independent valuation. It is important to understand there is a conflict of interest in an agent appraising your existing dwelling while at the same time selling you a home. If you are happy with that agent, it's okay to award them the listing at a later date. But do not purchase solely on their word in terms of the value of your existing dwelling.

The second danger inherent in an overquoting agent lies in the probability that the sales campaign will fail and the home will then languish on the market. When auction clearance rates drop suddenly—sometimes by up to 20 per cent—the market is clearly saying it won't continue to overpay. Four out of 10 people who go to auction expecting a 'bidding war' on their home fail to sell under these circumstances.

As the home languishes, the best buyers in the marketplace become spooked. 'Why hasn't it sold?' 'I wonder what's wrong with it.' 'The owners want too much.' And on it goes.

There is one type of buyer who is more than happy to make an offer on a stale listing—the bargain hunter.

These buyers love overquoting agents and compromised sellers. Here's a perfect scenario for people looking for a fire sale: The agent overquotes the selling price—sellers then buy elsewhere, and now they must sell—the campaign fails—the bargain hunter is the only person to make an offer.

Yes, the stakes are high when you call an agent in to appraise your home. Often higher than many people realise.

Protection

Now you are aware of the danger in being overquoted, you can take affirmative action to protect against it. Here are five steps you can take to ward off an overquoting agent and the dangers that ensue:

1. **Get a guarantee.** Have the agent guarantee their quoted price. Say something like, 'Before you provide us with a price, we would like you to know that we expect you to guarantee it. If it sells below the lowest price point quoted today, we are free of any obligation

to pay you commission.' At the very least, ensure you have the means to negotiate their fee down if they fail to achieve the quoted price.

2. **Seek evidence for pricing.** Whatever price the agent quotes, it must be backed by logic and evidence. If an agent can't explain and justify the price to the seller, then they have no chance of doing so to a buyer in the heat of battle.

3. **Understand strategy and tactics.** Focus on what the agent will do to achieve the price if granted the listing. Quoting a high price is easy. Achieving a high price takes skill, strategy and resilience. Ask the tough questions before you sign, not after, when it's too late.

4. **Keep a secret.** Never tell the agent what you think the home is worth or the amount you would like. That's what the agent is there for: to price the home. Many agents' pricing strategy is to elicit the owner's price expectation and feed it back to them as an appraisal. But, nothing improves value like ownership. Therefore the owner is not the right person to lead the charge on the value question.

5. **Follow the market.** An agent may have previously given a high price when the market was at its peak, but is that price still relevant? In fairness to agents, the market price constantly gyrates. If your last appraisal was more than three months ago, then call the agent back in to get an update before you purchase elsewhere.

An overquoting agent can leave you exposed to multiple dangers.

<u>23</u> Horses for courses

Real estate agents, like sportspeople, can perform better in certain conditions and struggle in others. Some of Australia's greatest tennis stars needed to feel they were the underdog before pulling off a truly memorable performance, while others shone when they were on a roll. So too with real estate agents. A good agent in a depressed market may not do so well in a boom market, and vice versa.

When the market transitions from booming towards correction, the same agent still turns up for work at their place of employment. It is almost as though they have a new job, though. In a falling market different skill sets are required.

As a consumer, you might jump to the conclusion that an agent needs more skill in a falling market. In a boom 'houses sell themselves', so it must be easier. The longer a boom persists, however, the more the industry attracts agents looking for a piece of the action. So, while property is easier to sell once it's listed, winning that listing in a boom is infinitely more difficult because of increased competition.

In a flat market there are plenty of listings, but buyers are scarce.

To illustrate the real estate industry's inability to manage these changes, consider the following service levels. In a boom, sellers are over-pampered and buyers are mistreated, with tricks such as underquoting and neglected follow-up. In a falling market, sellers are often mismanaged and mistreated, while buyers are coddled as 'cheques on legs'.

In a rising market, the agent's job is to increase the sale price. In a falling market, the agent's job is to protect the sale price.

Increasing the sale price in a rising market

In a boom, the market is constantly setting new highs. The record-setting price last week becomes the minimum price for this week's seller. Agents are usually dealing with situations where they have one home and three to six bidders on it. The game is not about 'will it sell?' but about 'how high will the price go?'

A good agent will have tough conversations with potential buyers. As an agent, it is much easier to have such conversations with buyers than it is with sellers, because buyers are customers and not clients. At the end of the day, sellers pay the agent, so they are the real clients, which explains why agents prefer rising markets to falling markets. In a falling market, it is not much fun having to talk a seller down to a saleable level below their initial price expectation. Indeed, this is one aspect of the work that drives agents out of real estate sales.

To ensure you achieve the maximum sale price in a boom, select an agent who talks in terms of high prices. Beware of agents who refer to clearance rates, time on the market, market share and other issues of self-interest that might benefit the agent but not you.

Stay clinical when interviewing agents, even if they continue to introduce peripheral benefits. 'How will you get the best price for our property?' and 'What is your selling plan?' are good questions to ask.

Generally, it is only after sellers have signed and realise the spot they have put themselves in that they begin to ask tough questions of their agent. If an agent can't handle robust questioning before you sign, then most assuredly they will not be capable of handling a robust negotiation after you sign.

The best agents are able to handle all types of personalities in a negotiation. A solid grasp of psychology is a significant part of selling real estate, particularly when 'market forces and personal finances' meet 'emotion and logic' head on.

The best agents also have admirable personality traits that have a general appeal. They aren't aggressive—they are assertive. They aren't careless—they are empathetic. They aren't ruthless—they are decisive. All of these contradictory elements are at play as the agent works the buyers up in price on the owner's behalf.

If you are tempted to think a public auction circumvents the need for these qualities, think again. Auction agents have to convince buyers to continue spending money upfront on due diligence merely to bid at auction. It may be easy to convince a buyer to bid at auction once or twice, but when they have missed out a few times, getting them back to bid again is difficult.

This is particularly the case when auctions have wildly exceeded the agent's advertised price guide, which is extremely common in a booming market.

Protecting the sale price in a falling market

Warren Buffett, the CEO of Berkshire Hathaway, is renowned as the world's greatest investor. On 28 February 2009 the headline screamed 'Warren Buffett loses billions'. The subtitle expanded, 'Berkshire Hathaway drops $10.9 billion in investor's worst year since 1965'. But during this period of turmoil Buffett's reputation as an investment guru was not tarnished in the slightest.

The reason was that Buffett was 'outperforming' the broader market in the worst crash since 1929. On the money markets, the best money managers in falling markets are those who lose the least.

If you were to go looking for a money manager who 'won't lose any money' in the midst of a severe downturn, you would be likely to employ an over-promising shyster. Whether it be in real estate or personal finance, the person employed to handle your affairs can only operate within current market conditions.

A real estate agent who promises miracles and boom-time results in a falling market is probably being misleading.

In a soft market, we see the reverse symptoms of a boom. Instead of one house and four bidders, the agent is faced with one bidder and four houses. This puts downward pressure on prices. Therefore the agent needs to sell the fundamental value of the property. This is how good agents protect the sale price on behalf of the owner. To suggest an agent can conjure up a bidding war at market price and deliver a 15 per cent premium in this type of market is fanciful.

An aggressive 'knock 'em down, drag 'em out' agent can also be dangerous in a falling market. An agent who puts completing the transaction above obtaining the best possible price will cause the vendor to shed tears later. Both the agent and the vendor should show patience in the negotiation process, and this patience should never be supplanted by pressure to make a hasty sale, just for the sake of achieving a sale.

The best agents are masters at highlighting and holding value against competing properties. The right agent for the right market will put you on track for the right result. It is really just horses for courses.

Only the very best agents are fully technically competent across rising, transitional and falling market conditions.

<u>24</u> Tenants out, furniture in

The time has arrived to capitalise on your investment. But when it comes to selling an investment property, it's frighteningly easy to lose thousands of dollars—all shaved off your hard-earned profit. Agents often suggest to landlords that the tenants be moved out and furniture hired in. The logic is that a better presentation results in a better price. The tenants' taste in furniture and décor could impact negatively on the sale and you can't expect the tenants to present it in sparkling, as opposed to tidy, condition for the inspections. In some instances, moving the tenants out and improving the presentation before the property goes on the market can be the way to go.

However, it's imperative that investors realise they will be losing money before they (hopefully) make money when they boot the tenants out on an agent's advice. When a landlord makes this move, the income stops and the expenses accelerate. Before moving tenants out for a sales campaign, run the numbers to see if it makes sense.

A lot of investors accept they will forgo rent for the duration of the selling campaign. It is the unaccounted-for vacancy period when the real financial pain can kick in.

In an extremely buoyant market the average campaign runs at about 28 days. In a normal market the average campaign is more like 50 to 60 days. Add another seven to 14 days of vacancy while the property is prepared for the market and the lost income meter begins to rack up an uncomfortable deficit.

The average settlement period once the property has sold is between 56 and 70 days. The fact the property is vacant during settlement is often overlooked by landlords when selling. The total lost income escalates to between 80 and 100 days' rent (11 to 14 weeks) once all is done and dusted.

This lost income needs to generate a higher sale price equivalent to at least 11 to 14 weeks' rent to have justified moving the tenant out. The decision to lease furniture drives the price required to justify the presentation higher again.

Hiring furniture for a sales campaign can cost anywhere between $5000 and $10 000. Add this cost to the income that has been forfeited, and the selling landlord is down $10 000 to $20 000.

In many instances, moving the tenants out and doing work prior to marketing produces the best commercial outcome for the landlord. In just as many instances, the landlord's increased costs and commitment yield a negligible benefit. Knowing which solution applies to your circumstance can be the key to making, saving or losing $20 000.

Agents love a committed vendor. In times gone by, agents encouraged vendors to spend thousands of dollars on unnecessary print advertising as a tactic to increase vendor motivation. Now that the internet has decimated print, there has been an explosion in agents pushing the 'benefits' of hiring furniture. Coincidence or not? You decide.

Before moving the tenants out for the sales campaign, run the numbers to see if it makes sense.

Manage the sale

<u>25</u> Coming, ready or not!

Managing the sale of your property is essential for achieving the best possible price in a stress-free manner.

The predatory playbook some unprofessional agents employ includes bait pricing, underquoting and overquoting, conditioning and 'crunching'.

The following sections will equip you with the tools you need to manage the sale of your property without falling into the many manufactured traps of the real estate industry.

When first listing a property on the market, your greatest desire is also your greatest fear—it's the early offer. Waiting for the agent to provide feedback after the first inspection is nerve-racking. Is the home presented correctly? Is the pricing strategy in line with the market? Will people like it?

If the response to those questions is favourable and a buyer makes an early offer, suddenly the nervous energy shifts. Is it too quick? How long should it stay on the market? It's still early—there's no rush, is there?

Many home sellers have learned that when you list a property in the digital age, the buyers are coming, ready or not. With the internet, real estate marketing has become close to instant. Within days of it being listed online, literally thousands of potential buyers have run their eye over your property.

In most campaigns, 75 per cent of the enquiries and inspections will occur in the first 21 days. If you decline the highest offer made during this period, you are essentially working in the belief that the best buyer will be in the 25 per cent that enquires and inspects after day 21 of the campaign. In fairness, that could sometimes be the case.

It's imperative to know the probability you are relying on when you decline an early offer. As a general rule, it is safe to decline an early offer that does not meet your or the agent's price expectations. However, declining a strong offer just because it's early in the campaign can, and often does, backfire.

Even in a strong market, nearly 30 per cent of properties listed for auction are sold prior to the big day. This is because the best buyers turn up early, bid strongly and move on if their offer is declined.

In making a case for why the early offer should be judged on the price, rather than the timing, there is one aspect that can't be predicted. That aspect is context. Every sale has a different dynamic. Knowing the rules of poker is different from being able to play poker.

Whether or not the early offer is played to the seller's advantage is best judged in context. A skilled agent who can actually negotiate will ensure the decision is made in the client's best interests.

An offer that's early from the seller's perspective is often one made after months of arduous searching by the buyer. This disconnect in timing derails many campaigns because the best buyer is sent packing.

Declining a strong offer just because it's early in the campaign can backfire.

26 The win/lose transaction— overprice and undersell

In a rising market, vendors can overprice at minimal risk. In a normal or falling market, however, overpricing often leads to underselling.

The opposite is also true. If you price at market rate, this increases the chances of selling above market price—even if the market is falling or flat.

Vendors who list above market price often inadvertently turn the best buyers off their home, which languishes on the market unsold. The vendors have unintentionally set up a win/lose negotiation: 'I will only sell if the buyer overpays.' Naturally, many buyers reject this equation.

Most buyers are reluctant to step forward on a home that has gone stale in the eyes of the market. Sellers are better off withdrawing their home from sale than allowing it to languish unsold and unloved.

Pre-internet, the vendor who deliberately overpriced and waited for someone to 'pay my price' had fewer downside risks in doing so. In the digital age, the advertised history is on record for all time. Every property now has a digital footprint, and buyers can easily access its advertised history. If your home is overpriced and unsold after a lengthy sales campaign, educated buyers have been gifted information that's crucial in the negotiation process.

The auction system offers no protection against failed campaigns. For instance, true clearance rates plummeted to 50 per cent in Sydney in late 2015. The principle of market price holds true regardless of the sales process.

Understanding the fundamental (fair) market value of your property is the key to a timely sale at the best possible price.

This principle is simple in theory but challenging in practice. Putting a market value on something to which you have an emotional attachment is difficult. Add normal market gyrations to the fact that some agents will overquote in an attempt to win the listing, and suddenly confusion reigns.

Understanding fair market value has the benefit of ensuring you don't reject the best buyer or, conversely, jump at the first cheeky offer that is submitted.

During the agent interview process, whenever an agent suggests a price, assertively insist on two points. Firstly, have the agent demonstrate the sales evidence used in assessing the price of your home. Does their logic stack up? Is their thinking likely to be accepted by genuine fair-minded buyers in the marketplace?

Secondly, remember to insist, in writing, that the agent receives no commission (or a reduced commission) if they get the price wrong. This will ensure they are thorough in their research and come to the table with belief and conviction behind their price.

As we have discussed, independent valuers are an excellent source of unbiased yet educated advice on fair market value.

Once you have established fair market price, determine whether that is acceptable to you. If it's not, it may be best not to list on the market at all. A failed campaign can haunt you in the future.

If the market price is one that allows a comfortable move, then list on the market for the highest offer at or above fair market price. This sets you up for a win/win negotiation.

Fair market price often creates buyer competition. Sellers want to negotiate, but buyers want to buy. The smart way to attract the best buyers is to price accurately and fairly. This maximises the number of bidders for the property, ensuring a win for you and a win for the buyers who are in competition against other buyers, rather than with an overpriced vendor. Buyers are more accepting of genuine buyer competition than they are of a vendor who is blatantly trying to 'beat the market'.

If you list at market price, you will attract the best buyers in the market.

<u>27</u> Underquoting

As property booms fade, the damage and pain caused by underquoting shifts from buyers to sellers. In a boom, a low price guide attracts an excess of bidders, who all compete vigorously. The sellers end up with a satisfactory price, one buyer gets the home and there are many defeated buyers who line up to have another go next weekend.

What happens when the price guide doesn't attract the promised crowd of bidders? Then the pain of underquoting is transferred to the seller.

When a low price guide fails to attract the masses, sellers face the ghastly scenario of publicly passing in for a previously unimagined low price. Any chance of a high price is destroyed if your home passes in for a low price.

To illustrate how this can play out, take the campaign of a townhouse in Lilyfield in Sydney's inner west. It was marketed in late 2015 for $1.6 million but remained unsold as Christmas rolled in. The property was taken off the market then turned up in the New Year with an auction date and a new price guide of $1.4 million. On auction day, the new price failed to ignite buyers' interest, and it was turned in for just over $1.4 million. On the following Monday, after the auction, the property went back on the market for just shy of $1.6 million.

This ill-judged fluctuation in price is recorded against the property's advertised history, possibly unbeknown to the owner. A failed campaign creates a damning digital footprint that can haunt current and future sales campaigns. When a property is put through the wringer like this, the sellers can achieve a good price if luck goes their way, but it certainly makes it harder than necessary.

As a boom turns into normal trading conditions, it's crucial to remember that the figures don't always tell the full story. Property statistics often have a lag time—buyers may inadvertently be assessing a previous quarter's performance rather than more current results.

If you allow your property to be advertised for a low price on the promise that it will fuel buyer competition, be warned it won't always go to plan.

During a boom, a sale was assured for the vendor. It was simply about the level of success. Now the easy money has tightened up, employing the right agent, with the right selling and pricing strategy, is required to achieve full market value.

An auction that stops well below the reserve price in front of hundreds of spectators (and buyers) is the surest way to destroy the value of your home.

Why would the agent advertise below the seller's reserve price? The simple answer is because they know the vendor's reserve price is above market price. Instead of being honest and informing the owners that their expectations are 'ambitious', they underquote to attract buyers to the auction.

When the bidding stops below the reserve price, the agents will often pressure the owner to drop the reserve price to 'meet the market'. Some owners can see through this low-rank sales tactic, and others succumb to the pressure on the day. All salespeople know the client can say 'no' 100 times but need say 'yes' only once.

If you allow an agent to promote your home below the reserve price, be aware that they may also pressure you to sell below your reserve price.

Accurate, evidence-based pricing is required to attract the right buyers to your home. The right buyers are people prepared to pay a good price for the right home.

Agents and sellers who attempt to bait buyers with a bargain price may get exactly what they asked for—a bargain price.

<u>28</u> Divorce, death and distress

There is a cynical real estate cliché that says 'where there is a will, there is a relative'. No matter how tough a real estate market may be, real estate agents know there will always be transactions due to life's inevitabilities—death, divorce and distress.

It is crucial to prepare for these darker eventualities, which can cause major family rifts or a real estate loss that could be avoided.

Talking about real estate in these circumstances might be uncomfortable and disconcerting, but it does not diminish the importance of the topic. There is nothing as frustrating as seeing a situation unfold where money and real estate tear a family apart.

Baby boomers were born between the late 1940s and early 1960s. It goes without saying, if there is a baby boom, then one day there will be a funeral boom. Any experienced real estate agent will tell you it is common for opportunistic family members to have the deceased's house and assets valued between the date of death and the funeral. It's often individuals who have minimal or no claim on the property who do so.

Most people handle the liquidation of a deceased person's assets with respect, while some don't. This is why it's crucial to leave instructions on how you wish your estate to be handled. The best wills are those containing clear instructions. Have a lawyer prepare a will and testament on your behalf, and update it if you desire or when circumstances change.

A will is vital for all people who hold a significant asset or assets of any kind. The younger generation make the mistake of thinking 'only old people die'. The only way anyone can ensure their estate is handled in the manner they desire is to prepare a will while they are alive.

Divorces are a reality of real estate that most prefer not to discuss. When the love of your life becomes your adversary in a divorce settlement, it is essential that both parties remain pragmatic and clear-headed in order to achieve the best possible commercial outcome.

Many people go into a relationship believing a pre-nuptial agreement is planning for failure, so it's better not to have one.

Different people have different views on such agreements. Given it is a question of personal values and beliefs, there is no right or wrong answer. You must make your own decision on this issue.

In a divorce settlement, if there isn't a pre-nuptial agreement to guide the process, take legal advice, but aim to resolve the issues amicably. The love may be gone, but emotions such as anger, revenge and bitterness create a lawyers' paradise.

Similarly, in the case of a de facto relationship, seek legal advice on the best form of agreement regarding any joint property or assets. When such relationships break down, it can lead to a messy civil action to resolve any claims, and the rules are different from those applying to a legal marriage.

One way to avoid expensive legal costs is to appoint a person who is respected by both sides as a mediator. Once accord is reached, sign a legally binding agreement that brings discipline to the selling process. Points of contention in a divorce settlement or relationship breakdown that flare up during the sales campaign can cause costly mistakes.

In divorces, it is common for one party to be particularly keen to sell while the other is reticent. It will be better for all parties if there is a written agreement before taking the property to market, to ensure everyone has a reference point if required.

Financial difficulties or job loss may lead to selling real estate under pressure.

If circumstances are driving you to a point of liquidation, your biggest enemy is denial. Many people on a path to an undesirable destination refuse to acknowledge where they are headed. There is nothing more devastating than having to sell the family home because of financial hardship.

A mistake people in distressed circumstances commonly make is to overprice their property as a 'get out of jail free card'. Regardless of the circumstances, if you overprice you will undersell. The property market will never overpay to compensate the vendor for their distress. Therefore it is crucial to align price expectations with the current market and not to set an aspirational figure that would make your financial worries go away.

We can't avoid the tougher side of life and the role real estate plays in it, but we can be prepared.

It's better to be prepared for death, divorce and duress than to have your affairs dictated by external events and third parties.

29 Automated valuations

Just as the internet has increased the availability of data, it has also given rise to companies and organisations that offer automated real estate valuations. Just type in your property details and up pops a valuation, as if by magic. But before getting too excited, read the fine print; those who take the time to check will often find a disclaimer around the accuracy of that figure.

In the fine print some of these companies suggest there could be a variance in the final selling price of between 15 and 30 per cent. That's a lot of variation, and basically an admission that their automated valuation service is nothing more than a gimmick.

However, many people see the headline number and accept it at face value.

Telling a buyer a property could sell for between $750 000 and $1 million won't do much to clarify the fair price debate.

Indeed, automated valuations are flawed on so many levels, it is difficult to know where to start in putting them into a proper context.

The valuation of real estate can be done accurately only by an experienced professional assessing each individual property on its merits. Data-generated valuations are prone to overlooking crucial aspects like renovations, improvements, aspect, standard of finish, presentation, defects and flaws, depth of buyer interest, sales that have not yet settled and the terms of sale.

If a buyer or seller takes an online valuation at face value, they are likely to make a mistake. A mistake they will come to recognise in time.

Let's look at a classic example: Ivan and Lynn were leasing an apartment in a desirable waterfront complex. It was so appealing they began to think of buying in the development.

As luck would have it, while their interest was high, their landlord decided to sell. The property was listed at over $800 000. When Ivan and Lynn did their online research, they were provided with a report that valued the property at $696 000.

They duly based their offer on this report, thinking the landlord was guilty of gross overpricing. They could afford the landlord's asking price, but they were concerned about overpaying, given what the automated valuation report had said.

The property sold in two weeks for well above $800 000. Ivan and Lynn were then faced with having to move out and confront the market reality.

Confusion can reign for sellers too. When three agents assess a property as being worth around $1 million, an online valuation that states the property is worth more can be confusing to the home seller. Who has it wrong and how do you determine that?

Automated online property valuations raise more questions than answers. They are marketing gimmicks.

<u>30</u> Confidentiality

Loose lips do more than sink ships. They may lose you bargaining power, unnecessarily lengthen your selling period and drop the final price to a heartbreaking result.

Nearly every buyer asks, 'Why are the owners selling?' The answer to this innocent question can have far-reaching effects during any negotiation process.

Buyers are always amazed how often an agent will disclose the personal details of their paying client, the property owner. A common admission is, 'The owners are going their separate ways' or 'They can't afford to hang onto this investment home anymore.'

Such responses from an agent to an inquisitive buyer are a breach of the owner's confidentiality. Sometimes the motive for selling is even displayed in the agent's advertising: 'Bought elsewhere — must sell' or 'Deceased estate'.

Properties are often advertised as 'deceased estates' because that carries the implication that it must be sold now, even if it fails to achieve the best price the market can offer at that time. This is a disgusting marketing tactic that shows complete disrespect for the property owner's family. It is a low-rank sales tactic that has somehow become widely accepted as normal. If you are ever given the responsibility of handling someone's estate, do that person the honour of refusing to have their main asset flogged off as a 'deceased estate'.

'Mortgagee in Possession' is another phrase that both banks and real estate agents allow to be plastered all over their marketing material. Again, the focus is on dumping the asset in a 'fire sale' rather than achieving full market price for it. And again it shows a lack of respect for the owners, who may have gone bankrupt.

One high-profile Sydney agent who is conscious about not breaching seller confidentiality uses this line to attract buyers: 'Mr and Mrs Buyer: read my lips. The property will be sold. I cannot tell you why, but the property has to be and will be sold on Saturday at the auction.' This is a line he proudly instructs his sales agents to use to ensure buyers turn up at the auction to bid.

The stronger the market demand for a property is, the less likely it will be that owners have to worry about their reasons for selling being used against them, either by an agent or by the buyers themselves. But why take that chance by letting your reason for listing become known in the marketplace and potentially used against you in negotiations?

Some people feel it is prudent to avoid telling their agent the real reason for selling. Their rationale is that the agent can't then use their 'must sell' circumstances against them. There may be some merit in taking such a position. The one thing an agent doesn't want is a depressed, unenthused vendor. If you don't feel comfortable levelling with an agent about the real reasons for selling and how it impacts on your circumstances, then find a trusted agent who does not employ predatory or unprofessional tactics.

In many instances, the seller's motivation won't really matter when negotiating the final transaction. In some circumstances, though, keeping an agent in the dark can backfire. If you are involved with bridging finance because you have already bought elsewhere, telling the agent you are relaxed and not in a rush won't help.

The bigger question is not whether to tell an agent why you are selling, but rather, whether the agent will then tell buyers. The best way to detect this is to have someone 'mystery shop' the agents you are considering hiring for the sale. Have the mystery shopper attempt to elicit confidential, personal information about the vendor. If they are successful in gaining that information, strike that firm off your prospective agents list immediately.

An agent with a fancy advertising campaign that discloses personal information about the seller and their motivation for selling quickly becomes a liability to the seller. This is particularly so if there is only one buyer for the property.

Although there are many competitive sales in a buoyant marketplace, most of the strong buyer competition is generally for properties under $1.25 million. The market has not quite rebounded to the same degree above that price point. Therefore it is still possible your agent will end up negotiating the sale with one buyer, and if that one buyer is armed with your personal story, your position can be weakened.

There is no doubt that competition affects price. Many people select their agent on the basis of a solid strategy that uses competition among buyers to maximise the sale price. Few people select their agent on the basis of how they will handle the sale if there is only one buyer. How do you have an auction with only one genuine buyer? How do you negotiate the best price in this situation? How do you avoid giving the buyer the upper hand by divulging information that weakens your selling position? These are practical questions that should be considered when assessing an agent's strategy and skill set for handling the sale of your valuable asset.

Whether you like it or not, an agent can win or lose you 5 per cent on your sale price in just 10 minutes.

Insist in writing that your agent keep your reason for selling confidential. By doing so you avoid any possibility of weakening your position.

<u>31</u> Bait price damage

Here is the Monash Business School definition of bait pricing:

> Advertising an item at an unrealistically low price as 'bait' to lure customers to a store or selling place.

When the market is strong, bait pricing by real estate agents is rampant. For a buyer, seeing a property promoted for $1.2 million or more but sell for over $1.5 million can be confusing. Is the market really that strong or are you being misled? That's the question many unsuccessful buyers ask themselves as they leave auctions defeated again and again.

Either way, it's tough! To spend money on checks and searches on a property that you had no chance of securing really stinks.

As a result of bait pricing, many home buyers are misled into bidding on properties they have no chance of winning at the auction. Furthermore, the owners have no intention of selling at the price point the misled buyer can afford to pay for the property.

In a common example, a house in Rozelle sold for $1 515 000 when the reserve price was $1.35 million. Great result. The only problem was buyers were told $1.2 million plus. That's a whopping 25 per cent between the quote price and the sale price, and a huge 12.5 per cent spread between the quote price and the reserve price.

Both buyers and sellers would do well to remember this point: the auction system cannot work without bait pricing. Now that dummy bidding is outlawed, bait pricing is the replacement strategy to fuel an auction with multiple bidders.

Savvy buyers will move to counteract bait pricing by refusing to play the game. They will submit their best and highest offer to the agent and state that they will not be attending the auction. They will send a copy of the offer to the vendor's lawyer to ensure the offer makes it all the way to the vendor.

Just because a seller wants to go to auction, it does not mean buyers have to take the bait.

If, as a seller, you are feeling uncomfortable that an agent is promoting your property at a lower price than you are prepared to accept, then you should be.

<u>32</u> Loss of control

Each weekend between 500 and 800 properties are auctioned across Australia's two most populated cities. Agents tend to judge the success of each campaign relative to the reserve price. If the property is handed in below the reserve price, it means the campaign has failed. If bidding reaches or goes over the reserve price, the auction is judged as having been successful.

Sellers are often unaware that at or above the reserve price the auctioneer can legally sell the property on behalf of the vendor. Once the auction reaches the reserve price, the agents are in full legal and practical control of the sale.

Therefore the seller effectively loses control of their property at the reserve price.

Many consumers are aware of the power an auctioneer can exert if required. As a defensive play, vendors may simply set a high reserve. But agents have many tricks to ensure the bidding and the reserve price coincide on the day.

Some of these tricks involve getting the buyers up in price and some involve getting the reserve price (the owner's price) down to 'meet the market'. Once the reserve has been met, if the bidding keeps going, great. If not, well, at least it sold.

If you are aware of the reserve price tricks used during an auction campaign you will be prepared and better able to defend yourself.

Here are five common tricks to watch out for.

1. Setting a high reserve can lead to intense pressure at the auction

While many vendors sign up for an auction with the apparent protection of a high reserve, most agents know there are several points in the campaign at which they can pressure a vendor to lower the reserve. One of those is at the auction itself.

If the auction stalls below the reserve price, the auctioneer will halt proceedings while instructions are sought from the vendor. Immense pressure is then put on the vendor, when everyone who has gathered for the auction turns and looks expectantly at them to see if they are going to 'meet the market'. Agents only need an affirmative nod of the head to drop the reserve price to where the bidding has stalled and suddenly 'it's on the market'.

2. A (low) buyers' guide becomes the reserve price

A low reserve will attract a lot of bidders. A price guide below the reserve price will attract even more bidders. Apparently the more bidders attracted to the auction, the higher the price, even though you attracted them with a low price in the beginning.

As a seller, if you agree to market your home using the flawed logic of 'a low price attracts more bidders and a higher sale price', be prepared for deceitful tactics to be used on you in return.

If the auction stalls below the reserve price, the agent and buyers will expect you to honour the advertised price guide. After all, 'you agreed to market your home at that (low) price'.

3. Conditioning and crunching

An agent conditions when they praise your home to win the listing and then systemically points out its faults during the campaign to drive price expectations down. Some agents condition subtly, while others are more transparent and crass in their execution of the strategy. This tactic is taught in great detail by some real estate training educators.

It's normal for a low offer or two to be submitted to the owner prior to the auction day. This is part of the conditioning process, softening the seller up for auction day.

The crunch comes if the bidding stalls below the reserve. The agent clearly intimates that the deal has to be done 'today' before we 'lose them'.

If the auction stops short of the reserve price and the agent insists you drop the reserve to sell today, resist the crunch. Sales books are also full of tactics for how salespeople can overcome 'No' or 'We want to think about it'.

Aside from the property not selling under the hammer, is it really that unreasonable of you to choose to think about it? In a rising market, the buyer is under more pressure than the seller.

4. Stimulating the bidding

At auctions there are often a number of bidders who will hold back until the reserve price has been reached. If the auction has stalled, agents will encourage an owner to drop the reserve price to 'stimulate the bidding' and draw out the reluctant bidders.

Agreeing to this tactic legally puts the property on the market at a price that the vendor would never have dreamed of selling for at the beginning of the campaign.

It is a massive gamble to drop the reserve price in the hope of stimulating the bidding. It is an all-or-nothing tactic from a vendor's perspective. However, it's optimal from the agent's point of view, given they get paid even if the property sells at the lowered reserve price.

5. The emotional buyer who's going to keep bidding

'We stopped bidding because the other bidder was just going to keep on bidding. They really wanted it!'

How many times have you heard this or a version of it from the underbidder? What they are effectively saying is that the property would have sold for a higher price if only there was another buyer around to fuel the bidding. As a vendor, once you are over reserve, you can watch the emotional bidder blast the competition out of the water. Even though it's obvious they would keep bidding, you legally have to sell to them when the second bidder stops bidding.

Yes! You have to sell to them even though they would have paid more for your home.

The crowd will clap and the agent will tell you how much over the reserve he or she has achieved. But you could have achieved more for your property had you selected a superior selling method. Perhaps it is worth considering that the public auction method applied to the wrong property may be the biggest trick of all.

Remember the predatory tactics used by some auction agents, and protect yourself against losing control of the sale.

<u>33</u> Tricks to increase vendor motivation

If you want an above-market price for your property, agents have a number of tricks to bring you back down to market price. Some agents employ subtle tactics, while others are more overt. Either way, when you know what they are, you stand a better chance of protecting yourself.

Here are five of the best-known methods used by agents to coerce a scale-back in reserve price:

- **The pre-auction low offer**. If you are expecting a huge price on auction day, an offer well below your expected price often surfaces about a week before the auction. The agent does not expect the offer to be accepted. They just want you to second-guess your price expectations and feel grateful when the price exceeds the bargain hunter's low-ball offer.

- **Moving the tenants out**. The more financially committed the vendor is during a campaign, the more likely they will accept the highest bid on the day. Encouraging tenants to vacate in the name of an 'improved presentation' increases the vendor's financial exposure to the campaign.

- **Setting a deadline**. Sellers are often encouraged to auction their property because the deadline (the auction date) can pressure buyers to act. However, as the deadline draws closer, the pressure of the situation shifts from the buyers to the seller. While buyers can wait for other properties to come onto the market, the seller is publicly exposed on auction day.

  Don't let a reported clearance rate of 80 per cent fool you into a false sense of security. Many properties are withdrawn or fail to sell at auction, so the 'result' conveniently goes unreported. It is well known among agents that the real clearance rate is always significantly lower than the figure advertised.

  It is important to understand that the agent's clearing a property and the vendor's achieving the best possible price are two very separate outcomes.

- **Hiring furniture in**. When an owner hires expensive designer furniture from a home staging company on a six-week contract, it creates both an expense and a deadline for the vendor.

- **Upselling advertising**. As you have discovered, agents are addicted to Vendor Paid Advertising (VPA). They often tell each other in training courses that upfront VPA ensures they get a committed vendor from the start. 'Premium package' internet campaigns are designed to lighten vendors' wallets. If an agent really believes in these advertising methods, ask them to carry the cost and risk of the strategy. You may find the agent can quickly deliver a buyer without either of you having to commit to a massive upfront expenditure.

The greatest losses often occur at the time of greatest gains. It's a reality that vendors are resilient and careful when the market is flat, yet more relaxed and amenable to expenditure in boom markets. If you stay resilient and careful, you can be assured of the best possible net result.

Know the tactics agents use to pressure vendors before you engage any agent.

<u>34</u> Selling off-market—is it advisable?

Sales that are not advertised publicly occur in both rising and falling markets, but are particularly common when markets are rising.

In exploring the merits of selling property off-market, it is important to look at this type of sale in the context of different market conditions.

Rising (strong) markets

Strong markets are marked by low supply and excess demand. Essentially, this means there are more active buyers than sellers. The main effect of this situation is that excess buyers drive prices higher by outbidding each other for limited housing stock.

When the market is like this, there can be advantages for both buyers and sellers in an off-market sale. Firstly, an off-market sale can save the seller both the effort and the cost of a full sales campaign. Secondly, the buyer secures the home they desire without having to compete with multiple buyers.

One drawback from a seller's point of view is that the competitive nature of an 'on the market' sale is largely absent when selling off-market. This means the major question facing vendors who consider selling off-market is whether they could achieve a better result on the open market. Selling off-market for a good price in a boom is relatively easy. In a buoyant market, however, the difference between a good price and a great price can be tens of thousands of dollars, if not hundreds of thousands.

Falling markets

Selling off-market in a weak market can be a great way to go. In a falling market, the supply of housing stock generally exceeds the number of active buyers. Knocking back a good offer in favour of going to the open market can be a risk not worth taking in falling markets.

During the global financial crisis of 2008, a number of prized homes were listed quietly with agents off-market. The owners wanted (or needed) to offload the asset but did not want to let friends, neighbours and the open market know their home was for sale.

Things to consider when setting up an off-market sale

If you want to sell off-market, there are several options open and a number of things to consider.

In a strong market—listing with an agent

The simplest method is to list with an agent while not allowing them to advertise your home. In pre-internet days, when agents were sloppy with their data management, this might have been more difficult to execute.

Back then, agents chose to hit every home seller for the cost of a full advertising campaign. As the old saying goes, they were effectively 'advertising this week's listings to next week's buyers, using the seller's money'. Despite constituting a complete waste of the advertising budget, this policy was brushed off by agents as nothing to worry about, because it was paid for by the vendor.

Today, good agents make a quick and thorough search of their buyer database to find pre-qualified 'select' candidates who might be interested in buying your home.

There are a number of agents across the country who actively promote their skills at quiet, off-market or 'by stealth' sales. The best agents are those who can produce lists of qualified buyers on demand. An agent who cannot produce a list of potential pre-qualified buyers before being granted a listing should not be given that listing.

In a strong market—not selling through an agent

Sellers who have a low opinion of estate agents can fall into a trap in which their main objective is to avoid paying a commission. Selling with a competent agent will, more often than not, achieve a higher net price than selling without one.

In a strong market, prices can easily exceed all expectations by 5 or 10 per cent if the agent has abundant competition at hand.

In a strong market, buyers who are unwilling to compete against other buyers often resort to prospecting for a home. Whether by word of mouth, social media or leaflet drops, a determined buyer will sniff out someone wanting to sell off-market. The sheer frustration of constantly losing bidding wars in auctions and receiving poor service from agents leads them down this path. A private buyer will usually promise a win/win solution for both the buyer and seller because the agent misses out on a commission! 'We can both save,' they will claim. Be careful of this claim—it has some traps.

A seller should never enter into an off-market contract with a buyer without having a very clear idea of the current market price for their property. The seller would be well advised to get a paid, independent, confidential valuation from a registered valuer before beginning negotiations. Never show this to the buyer or an estate agent. Once you have the valuation report, call in an agent you trust. Ask them what they believe the property could sell for in the current market.

Remember that a valuer's price reflects what, in their opinion, the property *would definitely* sell for, today. An agent will give you a price the property *could* sell for, if given the time to run a good sales campaign. There may be a difference between those two prices.

If the agent promises more than the private buyer offers you, ask the agent if they would be prepared to *guarantee* a higher price than the buyer has offered. You could say something like, 'As we have been offered $1 million privately, to justify listing with an agent we would need to get $1.025 million or more. Are you prepared to agree to no commission below $1.025 million?'

This question will quickly flush out the agent's level of confidence in the price they promise you.

In a weak market

One of the most justifiable circumstances for an off-market sale is where there is an expensive, prestige or unique home for sale in a slow, flat market. In real estate terms, 'unique' is defined as 'priceless' by emotional property owners. As you have discovered, unique homes often require unique purchasers, which are in short supply in a flat market.

Prestige homes in Sydney, Melbourne and Perth often sell off-market because even in strong markets the auction clearance rate of prestige homes generally underperforms the broader auction clearance rate. This makes selling off-market more attractive for these types of homes in any market.

* * *

Is selling off-market advisable? The question is best answered in the context of market conditions at the time of selling.

In a strong market, an agent's job is to get the best possible price for the vendor. In a falling market, while the agent's job essentially remains the same, it is also their responsibility to protect the vendor from accepting a lower than necessary price.

If you are going to sell off-market in a rising market, you want the right buyer and the right agent negotiating for you. In a falling market, a good agent will be able to tell you whether or not the off-market offer on the table is likely to be the best offer you could see for some time.

Before selling your property off-market, determine the merit of this type of sale in the context of the market conditions.

35 Protecting yourself from conditioning

Here is a definition of conditioning:

> A systematic process employed by real estate agents for communicating bad or negative news to the vendors to drive down their price expectations, after the agent has received the listing.

Whether it is shortly after you have signed a listing agreement or when your property has remained unsold for a lengthy period of time, you are always susceptible to being conditioned. Protecting yourself from this should start before you employ an agent. If you are mid-campaign and your agent begins to condition you, it can be hard to extricate yourself from that agent, particularly if you have signed a lengthy agreement.

Conditioning is most easily identified in circumstances where the agent bombards you with negative news about your home, usually disguised as buyer feedback. You know you are being conditioned when the agent offers few solutions other than to 'drop the price'.

Pat's terrace in Rozelle in Sydney's inner west had a damp problem. The lower level of the home was below street level, making it especially vulnerable to the problem. To rectify it with a significant damp course was quoted at between $10 000 and $15 000. Before it was listed on the market the agent assured Pat it was a manageable issue. He recommended the house be listed on the market in its current condition.

Unfortunately, the market was slow. A number of buyers considered making offers but withdrew once they had read the building inspection report.

After several months of languishing on the market, the agent suggested Pat needed to significantly reduce the price to compensate for the damp issue.

The agent's feedback to Pat after successive inspections shifted from cautiously optimistic to downright pessimistic. Comments such as 'the buyers loved the location and the city skyline views' morphed into 'the buyers are really worried about the damp in the lounge room—they said it's going to cost $50 000 to repair'.

The incessant negativity about his home was causing Pat great anxiety, which eventually tipped him into depression. He saw his property as his superannuation and was depending on it for a comfortable retirement.

Pat was convinced he was going through a uniquely unfortunate experience—until he read about conditioning. When he discovered a hallmark of conditioning was the agent who lavished the owner and home with praise before being granted the listing and bombarded them with negative feedback after listing, Pat knew he was being had.

To protect yourself from being conditioned by the agent as Pat was, adopt the following strategies before you sign an agreement.

Only sign a short agency agreement. One of the most powerful tactics agents adopt to set up the conditioning of 'overpriced vendors' is trapping them into signing a lengthy listing agreement to begin with. If your motivation to sell is high and the listing agreement is long, the agent has all but secured a sale. If the agent has overpriced the home, they will spend the next couple of months whittling down the owner's price expectations by giving them negative feedback about the property.

By signing an agency agreement with only a short exclusivity period, you can deliver the ultimate response to an agent who begins to condition you—you can fire them. It is your home and you are the boss. If you sign a short agency agreement, you maintain the power. If the agent insists on an agency agreement longer than 60 days, don't hire them. There is no such thing as a 'standard agreement'!

Pat realised his agent was conditioning him and was able to terminate the agent immediately. By good fortune Pat's exclusive agency agreement with the agent had expired.

When Pat relisted on the market, any buyer who expressed an interest in the home was advised there was a problem with damp in the lounge room. The buyers were provided with repair quotes, which quarantined the issue.

Some buyers withdrew their respective interest when they learned about the damp. All buyers appreciated the full disclosure, though. Pat and his new agent worked together to find the right buyer prepared to pay a fair market price in spite of the issue at hand.

Pat's home did sell for a fair price, because he and his agent were open and proactive. For Pat, the experience was infinitely better.

Before listing, ask your agent to outline the positive and negative features of your home, in writing. Then the agent can't use any negatives listed against your property later as 'new' information, designed to coerce you to lower the price they originally gave. Ask the agent directly, 'How do you propose to overcome those negatives during the sale?' Shortlist agents with the best responses to this question.

Select your agent based on strategy, not price. If your property is priced correctly, the agent won't have to condition you — they will be too busy negotiating with buyers. The reason agents have 'overpriced vendors' is that they overpriced the listing to begin with.

Unfortunately, many home sellers select their agent based on the selling price they quote. They inadvertently turn the agent selection processes into a bidding war. The main problem here is that it won't be an agent who buys your property.

If you select the agent with the best selling strategy, not the highest selling price quoted, your agent can avoid a bidding war when trying to impress you.

Many people become angry when they learn that conditioning is a low-rank, premeditated sales tactic. They are surprised and disappointed that their agent of choice has taken the conditioning path. The key to success is to insure yourself against conditioning before you employ an agent, rather than being exposed after giving them the listing.

Conditioning is a weapon commonly adopted by agents. Protect yourself in advance by insisting on a 'get out' clause in your agreement if you are being conditioned.

<u>36</u> Reading the play to manage the sale

During the sales campaign, your agent will make some key recommendations relating to marketing, pricing, or whether to accept or reject an offer. These are significant watersheds in your campaign and their importance cannot be overstated.

As previously mentioned, most people sell real estate on average every seven or eight years. This inexperience in such an important transaction can be daunting. Being aware of the key indicators that govern every transaction will assist you in determining the merit of your agent's recommendation.

Agents do not always have the luxury of being able to tell their clients what they want to hear. But by educating yourself on the key 'on-market' indicators, you can assess recommendations objectively rather than reacting emotionally.

If you can remain calm and objective during the campaign, it will help you and your agent to deliver the best possible result.

There are four indicators of the health of your campaign:

1. internet hits/traffic

2. enquiries

3. inspections

4. offers.

Every vendor wants to be at the point where offers are coming in as quickly as possible in the campaign. But offers are less likely to be made by buyers if the preceding three indicators are not aligning.

1. Internet hits/traffic

When newspapers reigned, homeowners would spend excessive amounts of money yet have no idea of the impact of this expenditure. Now online traffic running on each property every day can be tracked in infinite detail. Trends emerge to assist the agent and the seller as the campaign progresses.

Ensuring your property is presented and priced accurately will ensure online traffic is strong from the start. Good photography and a price that will appeal to fair-minded buyers are far more important than an expensive advertising placement.

Effective use of database mining and email alerts will see the number of online visitors viewing your home peak in the first 14 to 21 days of the campaign.

The old advertising maxim, 'Good advertising kills a bad product, faster' is important here. This adage predates the internet, but it certainly applies to online property advertising.

It is crucial your home is priced accurately and presented well online on day one of the campaign. You don't get a second chance to make a first impression with buyers.

Given that online traffic peaks early in the campaign, it makes sense that enquiries, inspections and offers follow while the property is still fresh to market and in play.

After 21 days or more, you will notice the online traffic viewing your house begins to tail off. This is not a preferred outcome, but neither does it spell disaster, particularly if you have a unique property or the market is slowing.

2. Enquiries

Good online marketing will lead to further interest and questions from prospective buyers. It is crucial that all of these enquiries are recorded in date order to compare with the web traffic and inspection numbers for the same period.

Attempting to send buyers straight from online marketing to the open for inspection can cause buyers to become disengaged. One of buyers' greatest gripes is being unable to speak with an agent about a property before or just after the inspection. An agent who says 'just come along to the inspection' is likely to have too many questions from too many buyers at one time. People who pick up the phone and enquire with the agent are serious.

3. Inspections

It is easy to fill a house on the market with a lot of people. But unless those people are active buyers, their presence and feedback is unlikely to be worthwhile. A good indicator that you are reaching the target market is when there's interaction with a buyer who has just bid on other properties or is about to. This tells you and the agent they are serious about buying. Buyers' feedback is useful too. You will not necessarily agree with it, but you can concede they have a legitimate point of view. Reasonable buyers who offer genuine feedback should not be mistaken for bargain hunters. The hunter highlights every minor fault yet reluctantly decides to make an offer, 40 per cent below the list price!

It is important to avoid judging inspections by the number of people who turn up. Ignore all feedback from non-buyers and neighbours. Look for trends in buyer feedback. What do buyers like and what are they resisting? If the only feedback you are getting from your agent is negative, you are probably being conditioned, rather than receiving a cross-section of honest feedback.

If you have priced accurately, the agent has engaged and followed up on all enquiries and the best buyers have inspected your home within the first few weeks, you are likely to move to the offer stage.

4. Offers

The more buyers engage with and submit offers on your home, the stronger your position in the ensuing negotiation. And vice versa. The key to getting a lot of strong offers early is to ensure that all of the preceding three market indicators are leading the sale towards a natural conclusion.

Once the offers begin rolling in, it is in the agent's hands to deliver the best possible result.

Disconnect

A deficit in any of the four indicators outlined here suggests that something may need to be reviewed. The key areas to look into are marketing, the agent's skills, pricing, market conditions and the presentation of the home.

The agent has some control of these keys areas, as does the seller. When the sale does not unfold as hoped, trust between seller and agent comes into play. The seller may feel the marketing is ineffective while the agent feels the price is deterring buyers. As the seller, if you methodically and pragmatically review the campaign through the prism of the four on-market indicators, the answer will emerge.

The on-market key performance indicators will help you assess the sales campaign. By doing so you are likely to have a more harmonious relationship with your agent.

Close the sale

<u>37</u> Overachieved and undersold

The reserve price and auction clearance are weak indicators of success when selling.

When the real estate market is strong, it's easy to confuse apparent success for genuine success. A lot of commentary focuses on the vendor's reserve price and auction clearance rates. Neither is a genuine success indicator, but both are being boosted by industry spin as evidence that all is great in the market.

To fully appreciate how a lot of conventional wisdom in the market misses the main point, it's worth examining the definition of reserve price and the relevance of the auction clearance rate.

Reserve price

The reserve price is the seller's bottom line—their worst-case scenario in terms of price. An agent's role on behalf of the seller is to obtain the highest possible price from the marketplace. Gauging the success of a sale in terms of how much the price exceeded the seller's reserve price misses the crucial point: What was the buyer prepared to pay?

Many successful buyers at auction secure the property *above the seller's reserve price* and *below the buyer's maximum price*. In such instances, the sellers have overachieved yet undersold.

The auction sale amounts to a public victory for the agent and a silent loss for the seller.

The owners are assured that the sale is a success because they exceeded their reserve price and the property sold on the day. As the market promotes it, the property 'cleared'.

At the point that sellers sign up for auction, they are reassured by the agent that they can protect themselves by setting a high reserve price. That way the sellers will only have to sell if they achieve a high price. So the theory goes.

Many a seller has been confronted by the second reserve price — the one they did not see coming and were not warned about. When the bidding stops below the original high reserve price, the auctioneer will stop the auction and 'refer to the vendors for instructions'. At this point, the sellers are faced with excessive pressure (in front of a crowd) to drop the reserve price in order to 'meet the market'.

Sellers reluctantly succumb to this pressure on the day. Only then do they realise that the apparent protection of having a high reserve price is no protection at all.

Make no mistake, the name of the game on auction day is to sell the property. The agent's clearance rate depends on it.

Clearance rate

The auction clearance rate is the most irrelevant and overquoted statistic in the real estate market. It's irrelevant because fewer than 25 per cent of all sales in capital cities take place by public auction. To assess 100 per cent of the market on fewer than 25 per cent of sales is flawed logic. Furthermore, agents are notorious for withdrawing and not reporting failed auction campaigns. If the only auction results reported are the properties that have sold, naturally the clearance rate will be high. When it comes to the clearance rate, agents are effectively cooking the books.

Another reason the auction clearance rate is irrelevant is that it's general in nature. The auction clearance rate simply tells you what percentage of buyers were prepared to meet the owner's reserve, or better in some cases. There are still specific examples of properties selling for less than they did pre-GFC. These properties sell and form part of the 'high clearance rate', yet the owners have actually suffered a devastating loss.

The fact that a high clearance rate and achieving a high selling price are separate events is overlooked in most of the market commentary.

To sign up for auction exclusively on the back of high auction clearance rates in a boom is to buy into the idea that the auction selling process is responsible for the buoyant market conditions.

Be aware of all the elements that can come into play. For instance, record low interest rates, increased confidence in the property sector, self-managed super funds, aggressive Chinese buying, a stock/supply shortage and low unemployment have all combined to put some sectors of the property market on the front foot.

To make the most of favourable conditions when they do arise, it's imperative that you distinguish clearly between apparent success and genuine success before selling.

Sign up for a sale where your marketing strategy extracts every interested buyer's highest possible price. Importantly, sign up for a sale where you get to decide whether to sell or not in a considered manner, not in a high-pressure situation where the agent is simply determined to protect their clearance rate.

High clearance rates benefit agents while high prices benefit vendors.

<u>38</u> The offer

Deciding whether to accept or decline an offer can be especially challenging for owners. There is no rulebook to follow on how to play the offer scenario when it arises. It all leads back to a simple question: how do we extract the best price without losing the buyer?

The answer, however, is complicated. There are no certainties in a real estate negotiation, but there are some principles that will help guide you through the process.

Market price

What does the recent sales evidence suggest? As the seller, you may have a target number in mind, but how does that number compare with comparable recent sales? Does the offer seem fair, high or low?

Once you have established this very simple rating of the offer at hand, you will have a clearer view on how to handle the negotiation. Never base your response to an offer on the asking prices or price guides of other unsold listings. Always base your response to an offer on recent comparable sales.

The most painful offer to accept is the one that is lower than the offer you previously rejected. Remaining calm, logical and unemotional during a negotiation is crucial to making the right call.

Context

Many sellers ask hypothetical questions before putting their home on the market. Questions such as 'What should we do if someone offers $1 million?' or 'What do we do if we get an offer in the first week?'

It's natural that the seller poses such questions, but they can be answered only in the context of the campaign.

An offer should rarely be judged against time on market. The digital age has made marketing real estate an almost instant process. An offer should be judged against the feedback and interest of other potential buyers. If the first buyer on the first day makes an offer on your home, then yes, this can be a very tricky situation. Make no mistake, it quite often happens this way.

The bottom line is you cannot plan in advance on how to play the actual offer. The offer needs to be handled in the context of the campaign. This is where the success of the campaign will often rise or fall on the agent's negotiating ability.

Format

There are three basic formats in which an offer can be made—verbal, written and contractual. By law, real estate agents must disclose all offers to the sellers. When an offer is made, it's worth remembering that verbal and written offers are non-binding. Only a signed contract with a deposit cheque can be considered truly genuine.

If you accept a verbal or written offer that crashes, it's best to consider it a non-offer as you proceed, to avoid making mistakes when assessing future offers. Be wary of the high verbal offer—easy come, easy go!

Competition

If you are fortunate enough to have multiple buyers for your property, the whole equation becomes simpler. But before becoming complacent about having multiple buyers, satisfy yourself that they are genuine buyers. Declining a contract offer in favour of a non-binding verbal one can throw your campaign into a tailspin.

Once a contract offer has been made, it's best that all competing offers are submitted on a contract as a sign of genuineness. Any buyer promising to pay more without signing a contract should be played cautiously.

Competition makes getting the sale easier; however, if you make the bidding process transparent, as in a public auction or Dutch auction, you can easily undersell. Competing bids must never be disclosed, as the buyers then focus on trying to beat the competition by $1000. Use competition and confidentiality to extract every genuine buyer's highest offer in a short timeframe.

Non-price agreements

Value for both parties can be created away from price. A potential agreement that adds value for both parties is worth exploring if it is close to being acceptable. Issues such as delayed (or early) settlement, release of deposit, leaseback, reduced deposit, inclusions or even some vendor finance on the difference can bring a negotiation together.

The more a real estate negotiation becomes about price, the less goodwill can be sustained. If you are horse trading on such matters, always remember to give a concession if you take one.

Pre– or post–due diligence

The pre–due diligence offer catches many sellers unawares. They accept the verbal or written offer and mistakenly think the property has sold. Suddenly the building inspection brings up a raft of issues that causes the buyer to reconsider, or the buyer's bank values the property for 10 per cent less than the agreed amount, scuttling the deal. Any offer made prior to due diligence must be considered an expression of interest rather than a formal offer. Treat offers pre–due diligence seriously but cautiously.

There are no rules

There are no rules governing making, accepting or rejecting an offer. The property is not sold or purchased until contracts have been exchanged unconditionally. It's common for the seller to ask the agent, 'How long do we have to consider the offer?' An offer is an offer until the owner countersigns a buyer's unconditional contract or the buyer withdraws from the negotiation.

It's a mistake to think a buyer will leave the offer on the table for a prolonged period while the owner chases a superior offer from another buyer. Complacency can bite during a negotiation, even in a boom.

It's worth noting that declining an offer does not guarantee that a higher offer will be made in the future. If you accept an offer, you will never know if your Alan Bond was going to turn up next week, so don't think about it.

The toughest offer to accept is the one that is lower than one you previously rejected.

<u>39</u> A good real estate lawyer

Like all trades and professions, there are good lawyers and conveyancers and some not so good ones. Whether you are buying or selling, the right legal advice can be crucial to securing your dream home. Reaching a verbal agreement and signing a contractual agreement are two very different situations. A good real estate lawyer will ensure you migrate seamlessly from the handshake to exchanging contracts without incident.

Many people scrutinise multiple real estate firms when selling, but put up with the nearest or cheapest legal advice for the same transaction. This haphazard approach can sometimes turn the process of conveyancing into a world of drama, which usually occurs at the most crucial point of the transaction.

There are two errors people can fall into when appointing a professional to do their conveyancing. The first is they don't know what to expect from a lawyer, so they look online until they find the cheapest one. Petrol and power are commodities that should be purchased on the basis of price. Lawyers handling the transaction of your most valuable asset should be engaged on the basis of competence first and price second.

A real estate purchase is a long way from a corporate takeover. You don't need to pay excessively for a competent lawyer to guide you through the nuances of the *Conveyancing Act*. A lawyer with experience and a track record of success in conveyancing at a fair price will ensure that your legal position is protected.

The second error many people fall into when hiring a lawyer is they hire someone who does not really want the job. Perhaps the lawyer takes the brief out of loyalty to the client, even though they specialise in other areas of law.

As an example, a good corporate lawyer does not necessarily make a good real estate lawyer, and vice versa. Yet if a client feels loyalty towards a solicitor who has helped them in the past, that solicitor may feel obligated to take the job on, even though they don't really want it. In extreme cases, the file is passed off to a paralegal or junior in the office and given little further consideration by the lawyer who was engaged by the loyal client.

Conveyancing is generally a straightforward process for a lawyer. But about one in 20 transactions requires the involvement of an attentive, competent lawyer when complications arise. Murphy's Law ensures that the transaction delegated by the lawyer is the very one that will most require the lawyer's skills.

If your preferred solicitor does not do real estate work on a daily basis, it is a good idea to ask them straight out if they really want to do the job. Then ask if they will be handling the matter personally. Such candor ensures that during negotiations everyone will be on the same page and you won't be left floundering.

A good working relationship between your lawyer and your agent is also crucial when negotiations begin.

Before a property can be listed for sale, the vendor's solicitor must prepare a contract of sale on behalf of the vendor. This contract must then be given to the listing agent prior to the property being marketed.

Once a buyer or buyers express an interest in the property, they take a copy of that contract to their own lawyer for review and negotiation.

In a competitive market, there is every possibility that multiple buyers will be trying to secure the property. Whether you are buying or selling in such a situation, the agent and lawyer need to work closely together.

For the seller with multiple buyers in play it's very much a case of the more buyers the merrier. Tactically, you want all buyers to be satisfied with the terms of the contract so their respective offers become binding upon acceptance. There is nothing worse than declining a contract offer for a higher non-binding offer that eventually crashes.

A good real estate lawyer acting on behalf of the seller will professionally and rapidly move all interested buyers past the contract review phase. The negotiation can then quickly return to the agent for setting up closure.

For a buyer trying to secure a property in a buoyant market, speed can often be crucial to success. Most sellers will take an offer on a signed contract far more seriously if the contract has been reviewed and negotiated by the purchaser's lawyer. The lawyer then provides authority to the vendor's real estate agent and/or conveyancer to exchange contracts without a cooling-off period—pending agreement on price.

Presenting an unconditional contract offer to the vendor can often be the difference between your offer being accepted or declined.

A good real estate lawyer won't be able to guarantee you buy or sell at the right price, but they will be able to put you in the best possible position to do so with a minimum of fuss and at a fair price.

A good real estate lawyer protects your legal interests without compromising your strategic position in negotiations.

<u>40</u> The pest and building inspection

When you are selling a home, if a potential buyer requests a pest and building inspection and the result of that inspection is poor, it can derail the sales campaign.

Genuine, unanticipated issues can be damaging. The buyer can conclude that crucial information has been withheld and the seller can feel as though the buyer is using a tactic to lower the price.

When selling your home, it's best to get a detailed pest and building report done before listing on the open market. This will ensure that buyers cannot bluff you with a bogus issue mid-campaign. Conversely, if there is an issue that requires attention, you can rectify it prior to going on the market.

Buyers are understandably hyper-cautious when making a purchase. They are committing a large part of their wealth in a single transaction, and they have no doubt heard one too many real estate horror stories. Subconsciously, some buyers will often double the bad news and halve the good news.

A poor pest and building inspection report can cause the buyer to reduce their offer or even crash the sale entirely.

Even if you choose not to rectify the issues, at least you are aware of them. The best way to handle defects is full disclosure to the buyer. If you allow buyers to discover negatives of their own accord, caution and distrust can build.

The law may state *caveat emptor* (buyer beware), but a more ethical, and savvier, approach for the seller is to declare openly, 'These are the issues you should consider...' Full disclosure builds trust between seller, buyer and agent. It also avoids the need for messy renegotiations when the buyer discovers the negatives you may have attempted to hide.

Most buyers can accept defects and factor them into their offer, but if there is the slightest suggestion that issues have been withheld or smothered, most buyers will simply (and rightly) withdraw from negotiations or overplay the seriousness of the issues.

If you do decide to rectify a problem with pests—particularly termite infestation—make sure you know what the requirements are for your state.

Such work entails a mandatory sign-off certificate, so understand these rules and question any suppliers about their work—particularly in regard to newer homes—before spending money on what could be an ineffective job.

Honesty is the best policy when it comes to disclosing building defects or pest problems.

41 The non-binding offer

Deciding to accept an offer is one of the most stressful decisions you will make when selling. Accepting a non-binding offer leaves open the possibility that the buyer can attempt to renegotiate once their due diligence has been completed, and this only adds to the seller's stress.

It's crucial you differentiate between a binding and non-binding offer during negotiations.

As the market moves from a boom to a consolidation phase, buyers will feel less pressure. Therefore they will be more inclined to make verbal and written non-binding offers.

To maintain your sanity, it's imperative you define an offer. An offer in the eyes of fair trading law can be made in writing or verbally. Agents must pass all offers on to the owners as soon as is reasonable. This includes unacceptable offers, low offers and non-binding offers.

An offer, in practical terms, is an unconditional signed contract with the agreed deposit. An offer in this format is as secure as you can get when selling. It is so secure that the bank will lend against the contract in the form of a deposit bond for the vendor's next purchase.

The rules relating to unconditional contracts differ from state to state depending on the respective conveyancing act. In NSW a 66W is a certificate from the purchaser's lawyer stating they have explained to the purchaser the terms and their obligations under the contract of sale. The 66W waives all of the purchaser's cooling-off rights.

Vendors usually respond more favourably to an offer where the buyers have waived their cooling-off rights.

A buyer who makes a non-binding offer is not necessarily unreasonable or playing games. Buyers are often lied to by estate agents about the true price guide for the respective property. The result for the buyer is they fork out thousands of dollars in due diligence for a property they were never in the running for. Understandably, this is why many buyers wish to negotiate in advance of spending money on due diligence.

If you are selling, there are some basic rules to follow when negotiating that will protect you from a renegotiation:

- **Fully disclose all faults.** A buyer who discovers faults mid-negotiation is likely to respond in a worse way than if they knew in advance of making an offer. If your house has building issues or your strata plan has funding problems, it's best to offer a buyer full disclosure in advance of them making an offer. Once the offer is made, you know it's made with the facts in play. If a few buyers withdraw, don't panic — they were going to withdraw anyway. You have saved yourself the angst.

- **Agree to a price, but not an individual's offer.** If an acceptable offer is made in a non-binding format, accept the price but not the offer. Respond via the agent with something such as, 'The price and terms are acceptable if the offer is put to us in a signed unconditional contract. In the meantime, the property remains on the open market.'

- **Be extra wary of valuations.** Since APRA's toughened stance on residential investors, an offer subject to valuation has increased risk. A non-binding offer was recently made by a buyer for $1.29 million, subject to bank valuation. The valuer assessed the home at $1.17 million and subsequently crashed the sale. Fortunately another buyer was found, but you get the idea.

- **Stay on the market until the sale is complete.** The best time to find a buyer is when you have a buyer. Conversely, if you accept a non-binding offer and close the campaign down, Murphy's Law says the offer will crash, leaving you stranded.

- **If there is more than one buyer, only unconditional offers should be considered.** Being considerate and fair to buyers is crucial to success in real estate. Always ask yourself, what would I expect if I was the buyer? Note there is a difference between expectation and hope.

- **Treat each buyer equally.** The buyer often hopes the seller will favour them in a competitive situation. This is unrealistic. The buyer can expect a fair and equal chance to bid. If you have two, three or even more buyers trying to secure your property, provide each buyer with a fair and equal chance within a set deadline. But all offers must be unconditional by the specified deadline. To accept a non-binding offer, dismiss the underbidders and then have the non-binding offer potentially withdraw exposes you to unnecessary risk.

Many agents will be tempted to claim auctions overcome these challenges. The statistical reality is that fewer than 30 per cent of all transactions occur under the hammer. Some are passed in (in 2015 the auction clearance rate in postcode 2041 was 56 per cent). Many auction successes are actually sold prior, meaning they are negotiated transactions. The vast majority of sales are negotiated transactions.

These are not baseless claims; they are market facts. In spite of the spin, the auction clearance rate in 2015 was well below 70 per cent across the inner west of Sydney and middle ring suburbs of Melbourne.

There is every chance you will find yourself negotiating during the sale of your property. Knowing how to play the non-binding offer is crucial to ensuring the best possible result.

A seller has not sold and a buyer has not bought until unconditional contracts are exchanged.

PART III
Buying

Preparing to buy

<u>42</u> Five questions to ask before buying

Buying real estate is a massive financial commitment for most people. It is a decision that causes both excitement and fear. To work excessive hours all week, year in and year out, to make the sacrifices to fund a property purchase, means the home represents far more than just bricks and mortar. Securing the right home can provide decades of enjoyment and comfort. But many buyers who do achieve their dream find it soon turns sour, leaving them with a bad dose of buyer's remorse.

Such regret is often the result of a rash or ill-considered purchase. A symptom of this malady is when you start to question the wisdom of the purchase. It can be prevented, or at least alleviated, if the tough questions are asked before you buy. You might not always like the answers to the five tough questions that follow, but they are best confronted pre-purchase. Asking them after the event will just cause worry and sleepless nights.

1. What if interest rates go up?

Interest rates probably won't rise significantly in the next decade. While lower for longer seems to have been the mantra when it comes to interest rates, second-guessing the actions of the Reserve Bank of Australia is best left to the experts. But what if they did start to rise more rapidly?

It's crucial to recognise that Australia's interest rates have been at historically low levels since the global financial crisis (GFC). Given the average period of property ownership is seven years, it's fair to expect to see higher rates at some point in that timeframe. If you budget for higher interest rates that never come, you are well ahead. But budgeting for a continuation of low rates and then being hit with rate increases can see your dream home rapidly becoming your nightmare mortgage.

If your finances don't stack up too well when modeled on rate rises, then consider buying at a more sustainable price point. Fixing your rates at current levels is another recommended strategy to protect against higher rates in the short term.

2.   What if the market drops?

The cliché goes, 'buy in gloom, sell in boom', but when there are boom conditions you can expect there will be a correction at some stage. The market may rise further before it changes, but all markets that shoot up dramatically inevitably experience a correction, whether it's mild or severe. Take note that a correction is different from a crash. Corrections happen regularly in the property market, whereas crashes are catastrophic events such as the US sub-prime crisis. Don't believe anyone who spruiks cheap claims such as that Sydney real estate never goes down or that houses in the inner ring of Brisbane are recession-proof. Property markets fall, and indeed have done so frequently in recent times. The premier Australian markets of Sydney and Melbourne have a terrific history of performing well over the mid to long term, but the real estate market is more volatile than most people realise. If you are buying a quality piece of real estate for the long term, you will more than likely come out in front.

Your primary residence should not be viewed as a tax-free investment play. If you buy on this basis, you will find yourself constantly sweating on the market and not fully enjoying the true benefits of home ownership.

If you can't stomach the thought of the market dropping in the time you own the target property, maybe it's not the right property or time for you to buy.

3. What if I lost my job?

Fortunately, Australia has experienced very low unemployment in the past two decades. But, as demonstrated with the departure of car manufacturers such as Holden and Ford, economic circumstances can change quickly. What is the plan if you do lose your job? Sure, you may get another one, maybe even a better paying one. What if you can only get a lower paying job, though? These are worrying questions, but they are best confronted upfront, otherwise they can haunt your personal finances.

Given the last recession in Australia was in 1991, half the workforce has never experienced a severe downturn in the economy. For those who entered the workforce in 1993 or later, a recession is a historical event.

We often see reports of rising personal debt levels, mortgage stress or inability to move up the property ladder. There are two common traps that young people who purchase can easily fall into. Firstly, they expect to receive pay rises in the years to come. Secondly, they don't anticipate or budget for the fact that having children may take one income out of the equation. The household's income will drop but the outgoings will remain unchanged.

4. Will the rent cover the mortgage?

Home ownership is about security. Owning a home—mortgage free—is the ultimate security. The reality is that not everyone will reach this phase in life before they begin downsizing. There is an interim financially secure level that everyone should aspire to, and it is one that can be attained.

Getting to the point where the rental value of the property covers the mortgage will offer surprising comfort. Knowing that the property can service its debt means that you will never have to sell and meet the market conditions of the day. If living in the property becomes unaffordable owing to a change of circumstance, you can decide whether to sell or rent. The key words are 'you can decide'. If the mortgage is well in excess of the rental value of your property, you will most certainly need to sell if you face unfortunate events such as job loss or increased interest rates. Before buying, find out the market rental value of your target property. It's crucial information.

5. What is current market price?

Knowing market value and paying above market value is fine, as long as you are conscious of the decision you are making. Many people happily pay above fundamental market value to secure their dream home. They know they will make it up in the long run.

Once you have consciously established market price, then decide what you will offer in relation to it. Some buyers will buy a property only if they feel they are getting it at or below market price.

Questioning whether you did or didn't overpay, as you show family and friends around at the house-warming, will only end in buyer's remorse. Once you have asked the tough questions about your purchase, it's time to enjoy your new home.

Ask the hard and confronting financial questions before purchasing a property.

<u>43</u> Auction bunny

'Auction bunny' is a common tag for a naive home buyer who is duped into bidding at auctions when they have no chance of success. If you attend a lot of auctions, you will often see them. The auction bunny reaches their maximum price at the auction before the bidding even hits the seller's reserve. Understandably, the aggrieved bunny walks away from the auction disgruntled and feeling cheated.

They often end up with broken property hearts and a skewed view of how the market is acting against them. They also lose thousands of dollars in due diligence expenses such as pest and building reports, strata reports and legal expenses.

Here's what happens: An auction bunny asks the agent, 'How much will this property sell for?' The agent gives the standard bunny-trap reply. They quote a price around 10 to 15 per cent below the seller's reserve price. For example, if the sellers want a million dollars, the auction agent will say, 'We're expecting bidding to start at around $850 000.'

Maybe the auction bunny pushes the agent and asks, 'Are you sure? Do you really think it will sell for such a low price?' Then the agent will respond along the lines of, 'The sellers are keen and will meet the market on the day. The market sets the price.' We all live in hope!

It beggars belief that business is done this way. It's heartbreaking, even downright infuriating, to see someone go through the bunny process. But welcome to the auction system as practised by thousands of agents. So how do you protect yourself against being the bunny at the auction?

As a genuine buyer, you must do your best to protect yourself against the bunny tactic before heading out into the market, rather than complaining about it later. When it comes to prices quoted by agents, believe nothing and check everything. The agents are right on one point: the market will ultimately set the price. But if you are lured to an auction by what seems like a low price quote, be assured you won't be the only buyer looking for a bargain. You and those other hopeful bidders have been hooked by 'bait pricing'.

The more you inspect, research and follow the sales results in your chosen area, the more knowledge you acquire. And knowledge really is power. If your opinion of the value is higher than the agent's quote, you have probably stumbled on a bait price. At least you know before you waste thousands of dollars on reports, checks and searches.

Ask other agents for their thoughts. They will have a fair idea of true value. Many times they will tell you the truth about their competitor's properties—they've got nothing to lose or gain. Be careful, though; some agents will run down any property that is not with their office. This is an easy tactic to detect and you should rarely be fooled by it.

Attend other auctions. Ensure you understand the bluff and bullying tactics commonly used at auctions. Don't be frightened. Decide what the property is worth (to you) and stay calm at the auction, or find a friend or relative who can bid on your behalf.

You can also make an offer before the auction.

Follow these simple but powerful pointers and you'll rarely be an auction bunny.

You'll find them at many auctions. Make sure you are not the auction bunny.

<u>44</u> Trial move

There is no doubt that buying and selling are stressful and expensive. We have outlined some of the costs—from stamp duty to legal fees—that eat into your equity and outcomes.

In most cases, people make a real estate move to improve their personal circumstances. Aspirational goals, whether based on moving up to a more valuable location, extra space, greater access to sought-after amenities or more attractive surroundings, are common motivators in our property markets. But what if that move does not deliver what you had hoped? What if the move is a mistake? The transaction costs are non-refundable. And now you face the choice of either transacting again (and burning up more equity) or staying in a property that makes you unhappy.

Over the next decade we will see a large cohort of the ageing baby boomer generation make the decision to downgrade from the family or larger home. Making the right move is the challenge, however. Perhaps the idea of a self-contained apartment close to amenities, services and medical care will seem like the logical choice. Conversely, boomers may be less pragmatic and look towards more lifestyle oriented properties and/or locations.

This change can represent an exciting new phase in your life, or it can be a regrettable mistake.

A wise proverb says, 'Never test the depth of the river with both feet.' But when you sell the family home to buy into an unknown situation, that's exactly what you are doing—diving in, essentially with no more than a superficial view, and hoping it all works out.

Whether you are a baby boomer downsizing or a young family starting afresh in a new suburb, there is one often-overlooked solution — the trial move.

This strategy involves leasing before buying in order to test the new conditions before being locked into a purchase or the sale of your property. While leasing a property similar to one you have considered buying in the same area, you in turn lease your existing property. If the move to the new location is a success, then consider locking your position in. You can now happily sell your home knowing that you are going to a better future.

This temporary arrangement allows you to check out all of the amenities and the lifestyle changes you plan to make in the foreseeable future. For instance, discovering that the 'vertical village' you were hankering after is a parking and noise nightmare, or feels too claustrophobic over an extended period of time, can alter your views about opting for apartment living. Moving into an area with an older population and few child-friendly services or nearby schools can prove disappointing for a young family, as travel times to amenities that are crucial for you at your stage in life are extended.

Most importantly, though, have a contingency plan should a new property not meet your expectations. There are countless stories of people who could not wait to escape the city in retirement and headed for the hills or the beach — only to find their isolation from family and friends a source of depression. What was great for a weekend away or a short holiday is a different prospect when you are living there full-time.

Some, of course, fully embrace such lifestyle changes. But if you are unsure how you will take to major lifestyle changes, maybe a trial move is something to consider.

If you decide to undertake a trial move rather than adopting the 'sell/buy and hope for the best' method, there are still challenges. A trial move means you are likely to move house at least twice and maybe three times before you eventually get settled, but at least you won't have burned up 8 to 10 per cent in transaction costs. And you won't feel like you're locked into an unsatisfactory and unhappy set of circumstances.

Consider a trial move to find out whether a certain lifestyle or location is for you. This allows you to avoid committing to a purchase that may ultimately prove to be the wrong one.

<u>45</u> Finding value

Searching for exactly the right property can be arduous, to say the least. Every purchaser would love to buy the property of their choice at fair market value. But in a rising market, fair market value is usually perceived by sellers as being higher than it is by buyers. Multi-bidder scenarios often drive prices well beyond fair market value, justifying the seller's price expectations.

Anyone looking for a bargain in a rising market is unlikely to secure anything. However, property markets do throw up value buying in all economic conditions, even rising markets.

Fair-minded home buyers and pragmatic investors are the most likely buyer profiles to pay a fair market price. In a rising market, they consider it can be worth overpaying to secure the right property. By the time they have settled in and enjoyed their first anniversary in the property, the market price is likely to have risen to above the price they initially paid. Even though they overpaid, they can still see value in a rising market. It just takes 12 months to materialise.

This thinking is also manifested in how buyers talk about their purchase. At exchange of contracts, they keep the price confidential out of fear that friends and family will feel they have overpaid. But by the time settlement rolls around two or three months later, the buyers are happy to disclose to the world that they 'grabbed a bargain'.

Some options for finding value

Slightly overpaying in a rising market to secure the right home is not the only way you can find value in the market. Several other opportunities can be seized if you know what to look for.

Poorly presented homes

It is surprising how many people list on the open market with their property presented in a way that detracts from its fair market value. The emotional appeal of the property is non-existent, and this turns most home buyers off. But there is something to be said for looking beneath the surface of 'the worst house in a good street or location'. A common scenario is a long-held investment property whose owner wants to liquidate the asset with a minimum of fuss and effort. The owner opts against investing in the best possible presentation. Buyers who respond emotionally to property can dismiss such 'ugly duckling' opportunities. But savvy buyers who look past poor presentation can recognise the value on offer. Let's be honest, even when agents tout a property as 'just move in with nothing to be done', the likelihood is that we will want to stamp our own taste on it anyway. So, for those with the imagination to distinguish between a poorly presented but sound property and a structurally unsound 'renovator's delight', this can be a good hunting ground.

Stagnant market

If the market price of your new property has neither fallen nor risen since your purchase, it is fair to conclude you bought it at its real or fair market price. Many investors understandably look for properties that are likely to increase in price. It is equally wise to look for properties that are unlikely to fall in price. If you purchase a property that maintains its value and offers a consistent and healthy rental return, you are likely to have secured a solid investment at the right price.

Unrenovated versus unlivable homes

Unlivable properties are often judged by home buyers on their state of disrepair. The best way to assess an unlivable property is to apply a simple formula:

Value of the property once renovated – renovation costs/profit margin = current value

For example, a site with a free-standing bungalow that is completely unrenovated may have an end value (after renovations) of $2 million. If the owner wants $1.4 million, is the property overpriced? The answer, of course, depends on the renovation costs. If you would have to spend more than $600 000 to bring it up to a value of $2 million, then the owner is asking too much.

Generally speaking, the market responds differently to properties that are derelict and unlivable, compared with those that are unrenovated but livable.

Home buyers often outbid builders on unrenovated properties, but builders often outbid home buyers on unlivable properties. This is because builders see the hidden value in derelict properties, while home buyers often shy away from the sheer scope of works. Only you can decide the level of work for which you have the budget, knowledge and stamina. It requires careful costing and planning, and is not a fast or easy way for the novice to make money.

Under-rented

Some landlords and investors willingly allow their rental return to lag behind the market. Their thinking is that a stable tenant at a slightly lower rent is better than turning over tenants at full price. While that may be a good option in the medium term, the downside is that a certain percentage of investors judge the value of a property on the current rental return. Always judge investment properties on their true market rent, not the amount of the lease at the time you buy the property. Ask yourself, if these tenants departed, what would this property lease for?

Interest rate movements

Interest rates tend to move in cycles. Broadly speaking, aim to identify whether interest rates are in a rising or falling phase of the cycle at the time you are purchasing. Central banks are fairly clear in telegraphing interest rate movements to the public. The only time they tend to cut rates without warning is when they are extremely worried about the economy. The interest rate cut of May 2016 was a case in point, as the RBA unexpectedly moved to fight deflationary signs in the economy.

Rezoning

Sydney is awash with stories of homeowners who band together to create development sites. In the process, changing a single dwelling site into a multi-dwelling one can drive up the value tenfold. If you are buying or selling, it makes sense to understand current and future planning for the area in which you intend to live or invest.

In the past decade, developers have profited handsomely from purchasing cheap, abandoned industrial warehouses and converting them into showpiece residential properties.

That cute house in a duplex you have just bought is suddenly being overshadowed by the 'boutique' apartment building that is going up hard against your side fence.

State governments are showing a desire to see high-rise development close to transport on busy roads. Watch out for such potential development sites and check with local government authorities about what might be on their planning application books or what they will allow in a certain area.

Grabbing bargains

We all love to 'grab a bargain'. There are three types of bargains—those driven by market conditions, those with vulnerable vendors, and dud properties.

- **Market conditions** may mean properties are trading below their fair market value. Whether it hinges on concerns about the economy or negative sentiment towards real estate, the market seems to be offering really good value. However, as in the stock market, most buyers can become spooked when they see that others in the market are nervous. Just as every seller wants to sell at the absolute peak in a boom, buyers want to buy at the rock bottom of the market.

  The best bargains are bought in depressed markets, not in the middle of a boom.

- **Vulnerable vendors** can include the financially distressed vendor, someone under time pressure, or the vendor with an incompetent agent who undersells the property just to get a sale and ensure their commission. Good agents protect vulnerable vendors, even in falling markets.

- **Dud properties** often sell for a bargain price. If you feel that you have bought a bargain in a boom, you are just as likely to have bought a dud or 'faulty' property. Whether it be an awkward easement on the property or a hidden building fault that is expensive to rectify, before you take delight in advertising to family and friends that you have just 'grabbed a bargain', make sure you haven't bought a costly dud.

Finding value in all markets is possible, if you look in the right places.

<u>46</u> Buying and selling off the plan

A housing boom often creates a building boom as developers look to take advantage of market conditions. Cranes on the skyline give the impression that things are moving and buoyant. It might pay to get on board and ride that momentum, given the demand. But you need to get the buying decisions right to begin with, as they will affect the outcome when it's time to sell.

Let's look at some of the behind-the-scenes machinations as thousands of apartments currently under construction across Sydney, Melbourne and Brisbane come up for completion between the time of writing this book and 2020. Many investors (speculators) will aim to exit (dump) their off-the-plan purchases, hopefully for a profit.

The salesperson selling off-the-plan deals will often provide charts, projections and promises on how the forthcoming development will perform as an investment. The reason buying off the plan is so popular is that some people have profited handsomely from this investment strategy and some will no doubt continue to do so.

But there are some issues to consider before entering into such an investment.

Casinos are profitable. They are still money-spinners in spite of the fact that people occasionally win. It is the fact that a few people win that attracts the many who ultimately lose. The temptation of a potential easy profit keeps casino revenue ticking over. And so it is with buying property off the plan. Many people who thought they were going to profit actually end up with a loss.

As a major development comes close to completion, it is common to see a number of the properties put to the market at once. Many of the investors (speculators) are attempting to exit for a quick profit. The market is flooded with near-identical stock at a single point in time, driving prices down.

If you do intend to purchase off the plan, it is wise to hold the property for at least two years after completion. This ensures you are not trying to sell when there is fierce seller competition. The larger the development, the more people there will be trying to exit on completion, and vice versa.

The exit may have been pre-planned or it could be due to a change in the investor's circumstances since they initially put their deposit down. Whatever the reason for wanting to resell, one thing is for certain: buying off the plan is a whole lot easier than selling off the plan.

Buying is simple. There's plenty of stock to choose from, the developer will often arrange finance, and the commitment and reality of paying the mortgage is delayed by a few years. Practically and emotionally, it's easy to secure such a purchase if you are an investor.

A favoured investment play for many is to buy off the plan with no or a low deposit, years out from the completion of construction. In the meantime the market rises, creating a paper profit for the 'savvy' investor. As completion nears, the property is on-sold for a profit...so the theory goes.

Most people who have bought into a new development look forward to settling on their new property as it nears completion. For a percentage of buyers, though, the settlement letter is the unwanted one they hope will never arrive. Those looking to exit the development before completion want a sale locked away before they commit to settling.

History tells us that in large developments resales by distressed investors usually appear on the market before the developer has cleared the existing stock. Very quickly, supply can exceed market demand, creating added challenges for a distressed investor.

The developer who had once been the 'friendly vendor' is now a competitor in the market for a buyer. This scenario has been playing out across Sydney, Melbourne and Brisbane since 2010. It remains to be seen what impact it has on the broader market, if any.

Reselling off the plan is usually difficult, not only because of unsold developer stock and added competition from private vendors (looking to avoid settlement), but because an imminent settlement removes one of the key advantages of buying off the plan—namely, that the purchaser secures a property at today's price, but settles in a few years at (hopefully) a profit.

In many of these developments under construction, it's an unfortunate reality that some people will be forced to liquidate at the best price available. Given that fresh developer stock is competing with private resales, it's fair to expect some downward pressure on prices of brand-new apartments. The trend is not a friend on this one.

Buying

The availability of excess stock is not necessarily an indication that the respective development is a poor choice. Indeed, truly savvy buyers often come looking for distressed resales as a means of entering these premier developments at an attractive price.

There are many benefits to buying an off-the-plan resale. The price you buy for is likely to be lower than that the property initially sold for, despite all of the gurus spruiking the opposite. In the short term, there is a higher chance of losing money on an off-plan purchase/resale than there is of reselling for a profit prior to completion without settling.

If 20 per cent of buyers who buy off the plan decide to resell as completion nears, this means in total, 120 per cent of stock needs to be sold to the open market. If the developer has failed to unload all dwellings before the resales begin to appear, incoming buyers can expect value to begin to emerge in asking prices.

Not every development takes this path, but far more do than don't.

Considerations

Many people are attracted to buying off the plan because they don't have to pay for the property today. That's fine, as long as you can *afford* the property today. In theory, if you are unable to pay the mortgage today on an off-the-plan purchase, don't buy the property. Before buying, do all your sums on your existing circumstances. Don't factor in pay rises or selling certain assets at certain prices to fund the purchase.

'Empty-nesters' can find an off-the-plan purchase appealing. They can secure their next residence today and sell in a leisurely timeframe. This makes sense as they are less likely to attempt to profit on settlement along with all the speculators who are trying to sell out.

To ensure you don't overpay for such a property, always compare the asking price with similar properties in the existing market. If you are paying an excessive premium in comparison to the broader market, you may well be overpaying. Developers will always aim to avoid having their stock compared with the broader market. But rest assured, if and when you need to resell, incoming buyers are going to compare your apartment with those in the broader market.

Funding the purchase is the major consideration for empty-nesters when buying off the plan. If settlement occurs in two or three years' time, you can't sell your main residence today to lock in at current market prices, because you will be left homeless in the interim.

On paper, the plan is to sell the primary residence as completion and settlement near on the off-the-plan purchase. In the few years between the purchase and the forthcoming sale of the primary residence, the market may have moved. If the market has risen, you win. If the market has dropped, you lose.

Locking into a purchase at today's price and selling another property tomorrow at an unknown price is a risk that must be considered. When it comes to buying off the plan, tomorrow does come. And it catches many people by surprise.

If the off-the-plan property purchase being considered were completed, how would the price compare with other similar properties currently on the market? Are you paying a premium price? If so, it's important to identify what features you are paying a premium for and to decide if it is worth it.

It is possible to buy off the plan and make a profit, but it takes good luck and/or professional expertise to do so. If you lack professional expertise, consider buying existing bricks and mortar rather than an apartment in a model on the showroom floor. It's safer.

The value needs to be evident both within the development and within the broader market to make it a compelling purchase with good resale prospects.

Investors have collectively lost millions of dollars over the years with off-the-plan purchases.

47 Photoshopping— what's fair play?

'Can we see the property in the brochure?' asks the naive home buyer. 'Yes, of course,' replies the agent, 'you are standing in it.'

Welcome to the world of photoshopping. The technology is so advanced that almost anything can be done to change or enhance a real estate photo. From disappearing power lines to a zoomed-in and cropped photo of the 'stunning view' from the bathroom window, photoshopping is rampant in real estate promotion.

Photoshopping can be used to great effect without being deceptive. Enhancements such as dropping in a blue sky because the photo shoot was done on a rainy day, or vanishing the tea towel that intruded in the kitchen shot, do not alter the physical reality of the house, but they do ensure the best possible marketing.

Insertion of virtual furniture in the empty rooms of vacant properties shows how the spacing of the room could work and feel. So long as the proportions of the room and furniture are correct, virtual furniture has merit for both buyer and seller.

Ultimately, it is the property that is being sold, so the photos should reflect the property in an honest and authentic way without materially altering or enhancing it.

If you over-enhance your property in the marketing materials, buyers will become annoyed and deflated when they eventually inspect it. On the other hand, when the marketing is a true and honest representation of the property, buyers will find only pleasant surprises once they inspect.

Delivering on the advertising is often rare in real estate. Make every effort to make the home look its best, but understand there is a line between best presentation and deception. You can impress just by being real and honest in the marketing.

Before going to market, ask yourself, if you were a buyer looking at the brochure then looking at the house, would you see the brochure as a fair reflection of it? Most buyers only want what's fair.

Online video is increasingly used to market properties. Again, it is a case of being aware that the medium can be used unscrupulously or deceptively, in such a way that a quite ordinary property can be dressed up to look like something it's not. It is worth pointing out that you are purchasing the property you see on inspection day, and not necessarily the property you saw in the ad.

Another tool for buyers to use is a viewing platform such as Google Earth. Bearing in mind that there can be a time lag since satellite images on properties were taken, Google Earth allows you to zoom down to street level at a specific address and to take a 'virtual drive' around the neighbourhood. What it will show is the style and state of adjacent properties, the streetscape, how much open space there is in the area, how close commercial areas may be, the mix of apartments versus free-standing dwellings, and the proximity to shopping centres and leisure zones. If all you can see is a large construction zone, a dowdy streetscape of poorly maintained properties and not a green belt in sight, then all the agent's marketing spin can start to unravel.

Beware of the over-photoshopped property.

The search

<u>48</u> Boomers move to apartments

The mass migration of boomers from the family home to smaller accommodation has begun in earnest. This shift is not expected to dominate the housing market, but it is certainly worth observing the likely impact.

As this demographic downsizes, the supply of larger family residences is likely to increase. Baby boomers were born between 1946 and 1964, which means a reasonably large proportion reached 70 in 2016. As the boomers age, the rate at which they vacate the family home will accelerate. It remains to be seen if the increased supply this is likely to create arrives at a faster rate than demand. If it does, this could have a negative effect on house prices.

In reality, it could be devastating for boomers, given many have their retirement savings locked up in the equity in their home. Confidence still reigns among them that the next generations are sufficient in numbers to support house prices at higher levels, even with extra supply.

As boomers leave their family homes, the trend has been that they tend to chase the sea and tree change, move to single-storey unit developments, or opt for the convenience of being close to the CBD. Apartments in particular, with their low maintenance and 'lock and leave' benefits for peripatetic retirees, have proven popular with boomers. This new entrant—the cashed-up empty-nester—now joins the traditional apartment seekers, first-home buyers and investors, in competing for apartments.

It is widely considered that price growth for apartments lags behind that for houses. But research published in the mid 2000s indicated that apartments in many markets were outstripping houses in rental prices. Investors will be interested in apartments for as long as this trend continues. Tenants have shown an appetite for apartments in prime locations rather than houses that require constant upkeep. Being close to work, avoiding treacherous peak-hour travel, is another plus for well-located apartments.

With a large majority of boomers considering apartment living, the days of apartment price growth lagging behind houses may be numbered. Unsurprisingly, developers have been quick to take advantage of changing trends as Melbourne's and Sydney's housing markets have gone vertical in the past decade.

There has been a boom in new apartments that appears set to continue. As with most booms, the trick is to ensure it does not cross over into a bubble. A chronic oversupply of apartments would be a bubble no one would want to see burst. Real estate oversupply and cheap finance were the precursors to the financial disasters played out in the US and Europe in 2008.

As a result of the housing boom and bust of 2002–2008 in Ireland, the main form of construction work for a period was pulling down the newly built developments sitting dormant around the country. These estates were referred to as 'ghost estates'. It is highly unlikely Australia would experience anything like this, particularly in the main capital cities. But if you take a close look at sea change hotspots such as the Gold Coast and the Sunshine Coast, rampant oversupply is obvious at different stages of the property cycle.

Exactly how these changes will affect the housing market is not entirely certain. It is not a question of whether the ageing baby boomers will impact housing, but of how. As we have witnessed for the past 60 years, whenever the boomer generation has acted universally, it creates a boom.

Baby boomers have become active in the apartment market.

<u>49</u> Inspecting the strata books

As more apartments are constructed, many people will be moving into strata living arrangements for the first time.

Living in a 'vertical village' comes with its own set of legal, financial and social rules, which you need to understand before entering this sector of the market.

If you are purchasing a strata title property, it's crucial that you buy into both a good apartment and a well-managed building. Many people mistakenly make their purchasing decision exclusively on the merits of the apartment. The importance of buying into a harmoniously run, financially sound development is one of the most underrated aspects of apartment living. Adjusting to apartment living can be difficult enough without the added worry of a strata in crisis.

If 'crisis' sounds overdramatic when describing what can go wrong in strata living, rest assured it is not. Whether you are a first-home buyer, an investor or a downsizing baby boomer, inspecting the strata books is more important than the brand of oven in the apartment.

The standard of maintenance and presentation of the overall strata plan will be largely determined by the decisions of a voluntary owners' committee.

Fortunately, a vast amount of information is available on strata scheme governance and the legislation that applies in each state and territory. Arming yourself with this knowledge puts you in a better position to seek the vital financial, governance and lifestyle information to make a competent purchasing decision.

You can request a strata report that will advise you where the scheme's records and financial statements can be obtained; who the management committee members and managing agents are; what levies are required to be paid by owners; if there are outstanding levies; and what by-laws are in place for the overall property.

Given you are buying into a building in which you will share amenities and expenses, it is worth knowing of any issues that have arisen in the past. Here are some common issues to be aware of in strata schemes.

By-laws

Each scheme sets its own rules. This set of by-laws outlines issues such as parking allocation, what you can and can't do to your unit or apartment, whether you can keep a pet, and how any common areas can or cannot be used. Trying to change the rules after you have moved in can be difficult.

Noisy neighbours/conflict resolution

Neighbours are an underestimated aspect of buying a property, be it a house or an apartment. Before buying, knock on a few doors and meet the neighbours. They will soon tell you things the agent hasn't. In most strata schemes you will find a mix of owner/occupiers and tenants. Increasingly, too, there are short-stay arrangements associated with the growth of online sites such as Airbnb. Ask the neighbours if they have experienced any problems in this regard.

Well-run management committees should have provisions in place for resolving conflict issues and enforcing by-laws.

Les bought his apartment in Hobart to enjoy a quiet lifestyle and escape the day-to-day maintenance of a house. Soon after moving in, he met the neighbours, one of whom he clashed with. Their relationship became untenable from Les's perspective. He sold the apartment within 12 months of purchasing it, for less than he paid. Furthermore, the stamp duty and selling costs were a write-off.

Unpaid levies/insufficient money in the sinking fund

A few non-payers in a building can quickly cause financial stress in a strata title situation, particularly in a smaller block. In a block of four units, if two owners are behind on their strata rates, then 50 per cent of the income is missing. The pressure quickly mounts.

If you are in a negotiation where the owner you are buying from is behind in the strata rates, rest assured you don't inherit that debt. Those outstanding funds will be reconciled at settlement of the sale.

While these are common pressure points where things go wrong, you shouldn't jump at shadows. Most agents now disclose the strata/building levies in their marketing. When you find a property that has abnormally low strata rates, keep in mind that if they are collecting insufficient funds to run the entire building, ultimately the owners will need to pay a special levy of some kind in the event that urgent or major works are required.

Many strata schemes look for points of difference in their sales campaigns and offer numerous 'lifestyle' attractions. If, for example, an indoor pool and gym is something you will regularly use, or a roof garden appeals, or there are attractive communal socialising spaces, then they are part of what you are paying for and will continue to pay to keep maintained. Seeking to reduce levies after the event because you don't use those facilities is a futile exercise.

As a potential buyer inspecting the strata's books, you are entitled to see the financials to gain a full and proper perspective of how it is being managed. If you don't understand financial reporting, employ someone who does to give you the vital information you need.

Concrete cancer

Many units built between the 1950s and the 1980s experience concrete cancer. It is common for people to disregard a building inspection and/or engineer's report on a strata title property based on the idea that the strata committee has to deal with such issues. If you are buying into a building that is at high risk of concrete cancer, it's preferable to know this before purchasing. Conversely, if a building has had concrete cancer and it has been dealt with comprehensively, that augurs well for the future of that property.

Defects in newly built apartments

The flip side to the construction boom in apartments is that we will also see a 'defect boom'.

Defects are a reality of new constructions. You won't read about it in the brochure at the time of buying off the plan, though. Know your rights prior to signing a contract.

Depending on how the contract is written, the developer may have more freedom than you imagined. In extreme cases, the developers have changed the floor plan and/or the standard of fittings on unsuspecting buyers. Have a good real estate lawyer independent of the developer read the terms of the contract to you.

If buying off the plan, be sure to find out whether the developer will have an influence on the strata committee. In the past, some developers have controlled the strata committee until the builder's warranty insurance expires. If any defects are brought to the strata committee's attention, they waive the concern away until the developer is in the clear from the warranty. Once the insurance expires, the cost and risk of the respective issue reverts to the owners of the strata.

Many millions of dollars have been spent on court cases between developers and strata complexes in recent years. During the court case it is common for the market to heavily discount the value of properties within the development that are put up for sale.

At Glebe Gardens, in Glebe, NSW, the owners' committee was involved in litigation with the developer for several years. In that time, owners had to discount their prices by up to 20 per cent to the mainstream market. Even then the properties were hard to sell, such was the market resistance to the court case.

Fortunately, once the court case was resolved, the properties returned to full and fair value.

Special levies to fund capital expenditure

Special levies arise when there are necessary works required and insufficient funds in the accounts. A special levy, in itself, is not a reason to avoid buying a property, but such a levy, or the intention to strike one, is definitely a reason to investigate matters further. Depending on the scope of works being proposed, the special levy could be paid in one amount or over several quarterly payments. The works that the special levy intends to fund fall into two categories—remedial works or capital improvements.

In regard to capital works, a $10 000 or $20 000 special levy can add substantially to each property. Many of the apartment blocks built between the 1950s and the 1980s are now modernising their façades. This can bring about great improvements to the collective asset and in turn to the units within it.

One older apartment block in Drummoyne, NSW, was dated and somewhat unsightly when compared with its contemporary peers. The owners agreed to a modernisation of the building's face and common areas. The works were funded through a series of special levies. The result was a stunning transformation that added a financial windfall on the investment of the special levy to each of the owners.

* * *

These points don't serve as a complete review of strata title issues. Nor are they designed to frighten anyone out of buying into strata. Similar issues can arise with houses too. But given so many Australians will move into apartments for the first time in the decade to come, being aware of the potential issues is paramount. Hopefully you agree it is a mistake simply to outsource the necessary strata report to your lawyer or conveyancer when buying a unit.

Find out how strata schemes work and what due diligence is required for a successful buying outcome.

<u>50</u> Strata fees weigh on boomers

The baby boomer demographic mainly comprises empty-nesters. The children have moved out and generally come back to visit sporadically. The space and facilities required when they were all still 'in the nest' have now become surplus to requirements.

Many have seen a phenomenal increase in the value of their home, persuading them to enter the market sooner than they otherwise would have. They have seen this windfall as similar to having a second superannuation fund.

One thing that has surprised many in the real estate industry, though, is that despite long-held predictions that baby boomers would leave the capital cities in droves for the ultimate sea change, many are opting instead to downsize but remain in the city.

Well-positioned, modern apartments close to the CBD and its infrastructure appear to be their preference. These tend to offer superior appointments compared with older-style buildings, which were not built to modern lifestyle specifications. Superior amenities, however, often mean higher strata levies and fees.

A big consideration for many boomers in the future will be the ongoing fees and levies they will pay over the long term. While rates and levies may be manageable for those who still earn an income, they can suddenly become burdensome once retirement arrives and the big incomes stop. For example, quarterly strata levies of $3000 will add up to $120 000 over 10 years, without allowing for any increases or inflation. This could be a crippling financial burden for some.

Buying a city apartment

It is logical that apartment complexes offering high-end amenities are usually the most expensive. Gymnasiums, spas, saunas, roof gardens, concierges and elevators are all features that drive strata levies higher on a continuing basis.

If fees and levies seem high at the time of purchase, the confronting reality is that they are the lowest they are ever likely to be. Strata levies tend to go up not down, as do council rates. Furthermore, if a building develops a serious structural or tenancy issue, the strata committee may impose a special levy to fund works or shortfalls not budgeted for.

Take the time to understand how the management of a strata scheme works and what your role in it is. Well-managed schemes are those that are not only mindful of your democratic rights and asset enhancement as an owner, but are also dedicated to improving the value of the collective asset.

Buying off the plan

Buying off the plan can raise challenges for those seeking clarity on their financial affairs. The expected price of strata levies is not always clear with off-the-plan purchases. Even when they seem clear, there is plenty of scope for those fees to be increased if need be. An established building with a good trading history is usually much more predictable in its levies.

Boomers heading into apartment living will always benefit from weighing up the cost of strata fees and taking inflation into account over the full term of their expected ownership. The only thing worse than knowing about expenses is not knowing about them.

Non-luxury type apartment buildings where strata fees are lower will hold obvious appeal for many baby boomers downsizing in the future. Developers would be well advised to cater for the normal baby boomer apartment market as well as the high-end market. Too many newly constructed high-rises have been overloaded with features that drive the running costs of the building up for the benefit of only a few in the building.

If you plan to retire in a luxury apartment, carefully consider the ongoing impact to your finances of high strata levies.

<u>51</u> Profitable renovations

When the time comes to sell a property, any money you put into it should be deemed as an investment. This applies even if you have bought an unrenovated property that you intend to get to work on and then resell.

The purpose of investing any money is to make a profit, so each dollar invested into the property should be linked to profit. Many people make the error of putting a brand-new kitchen with high-quality appointments into the home just before they go to market. The new kitchen may improve the sale price, but if a $50 000 kitchen adds $60 000 in value, is the effort, cost and stress worth it? Often the $50 000 kitchen adds only $30 000 or $40 000 to the end price, making the investment a loss.

A number of television shows feature people making home renovations. They are entertaining with a dose of stress and drama thrown in to keep the audience engaged. To prove the point that renovations are not all high times and high profits, take the results from *The Block* over a five-year period, between 2010 and 2015. When the properties have a commercial reserve price set (that is, purchase price and costs + renovation costs), the auction often fails to meet the reserve. Only when there is an artificially low reserve does *The Block* look like fun.

Who will forget the devastated contestants in the 2014 series who gave up three months of their lives to win … nothing. This happens every day in the real world, where renovators are not given free labour and subsidised product from sponsors. Keep in mind that good television and renovation profits are separate entities.

Profitable renovations fall into two categories: works that can be done below retail cost and retail-priced works that add value beyond cost.

Works below retail cost

Many renovations add around $1 for every dollar invested into the property. If you are undergoing a structural renovation, to create true and meaningful profit from the works, you need to be able to get the works completed at a lower price than a builder would charge a client. The amount you save on the works will flow through as profit on the end product.

This is why many developers/builders do so well out of unrenovated/unlivable properties. There is a huge potential upside in the dwelling and they can get the works done at a price that produces profit. The disrepair of the property frightens most, if not all, home buyers who plan to pay the retail price on the works.

Retail-priced works that add value beyond cost

Most people other than builders fit into the retail-paying category, but some works can still generate huge value and profit. If you employ a painter to paint the house for $15 000, it will commonly add $30 000 or $40 000 in value. As a general rule of thumb, painting, carpeting and landscaping are works that will create profit beyond the cost of works.

A common scenario is to race ahead with extensions. That basic weatherboard or single-fronted terrace will be transformed with the addition of a second storey, or by building a whole new living space off the back. The popularity of such a move is evidenced by the number of operators specialising in extensions. The reality is that such building works can work out to be more expensive per square metre than building a whole new house. For the builder, they are often as time consuming as a new dwelling, but with less profit.

Cutting corners on extensions is not uncommon. The workmanship, quality and design being offered need to be carefully researched. Often a raft of costly and unforeseen variations pop up because other parts of the structure are in poor condition or need bolstering to carry the extension. Plenty end up looking 'tacked on', a mismatch with the original structure, and are likely to be viewed as such when it comes time to sell. On the other hand, a subtle, well-designed and properly costed addition that delivers a seamless flow in the home's living space can be a 'wow' factor that assists in delivering a fantastic result.

Market growth often masks the true impact of renovation costs. If you plan to do profitable renovations before selling, work out on paper any market growth in that time as a bonus. Relying on market growth to fill the hole left by the renovation costs is not a fun space to be in.

There are numerous 'property gurus' who charge you for the privilege of attending their seminars that promise to 'make you rich from real estate'. A cautionary and common tale of woe involves one young couple who staked the equity in their primary residence to undertake a renovation purchase. They did so based on advice gained at a property seminar.

It was going to be easy. They had been given 'the game plan' that would lead to inevitable success and profit. One of them had carpentry skills, so they could do most of the work themselves. They excitedly bought an older, three-bedroom, brick veneer home in a Melbourne bayside suburb that had seen some sections enjoying price growth while others showed little or no growth. They paid $380 000 for the property in the lowest growth zone, but once stamp duty was applied it was around $400 000. They had borrowed this amount, plus extra for the renovations required. With the outside rendered, a new front fence, landscaping, a wall knocked out to increase living space, a new kitchen, an upgraded bathroom and the addition of an en suite, their 'property guru' assured them they would get at least $500 000 on the resale.

It had to be turned around in under 12 months or they couldn't keep up with the ongoing costs and repayments. The costs began to blow out from day one. In addition to their day jobs, this couple was working until midnight, seven days a week, just to get things completed. Once the job was finished and ready for sale, their costs had put them in a position where they would be lucky to break even at the current market price.

The home languished on the market for six months, with the highest offer coming in at $410 000. Even the market rate of rent for the area would not cover their costs in the interim. Ultimately they had to not only take what they could get for the 'investment', but to sell their primary residence to pay back hefty loans. To add insult to injury, they had paid $6000 to attend the property seminar.

This is not an isolated case. Unless you are a professional in the building industry, most profitable renovations tend to be of a cosmetic nature.

Profitable renovations that involve development applications and structural works are best left to builders, tradesmen and experts.

52 Investing in the investment

Maintenance is often viewed as an expense by landlords, an unwanted and often unplanned one at that. However, it's best to treat money spent on maintenance as an investment rather than an expense. Expenses don't offer a return on investment: the money is gone forever once the expense is paid.

Maintenance really is an investment in your investment property that will either make, save or earn you extra income into the future.

This makes it even more important to get the investment purchase right in the first place, especially with free-standing property. The goal is a good rental yield while the property appreciates in value. When there are rental shortages, good agents will increase and maximise the price. It might have been advertised at $400 a week, but a tenant who offers to up that to $450 can create competition. It is therefore tempting to think that tenants are desperate enough to rent just about anything. These days, though, tenants enjoy a lot of rights, the most fundamental of which is that they are entitled to expect a property in clean, safe, livable condition with fixed appliances and amenities in good working order.

If your investment has plumbing and wiring that need constant attention, a heating system that is on its last legs, cooking appliances that are ready for the tip, and steps or stairs that guarantee a tumble at some point, then expect your wallet to be constantly open.

Tenants who are sometimes the cause of those costly maintenance issues can be highly demanding when it comes to rectifications. Let's look at one example.

This investment property had been brought to good rentable condition, including new kitchen appliances, new paint throughout, repolished floors, a new toilet suite, neutral blinds and curtains, and a garden in good, maintainable order. The tenants had been left with clear instructions that the property relied on tank water, with no mains water connections in the area, and what this meant in regard to how it operated. After the third occasion in as many months that a plumber had to be called to unblock the system, the owners had to take the agent to task for simply calling a plumber at their expense rather than pointing the tenants back to their own liability. A service agent had been called twice because the oven 'wasn't working'. (It was, but the tenants had failed to read the operating instructions properly.) Getting maintenance issues crystal clear with the rental agent from the beginning is vital if you don't want to see your time and costs blow out.

Make money through maintenance

Maintenance and repairs will make your property more valuable and ensure the value rises on trend with the broader market, if not above it. Buyers can usually tell the difference between a treasured home and a long-term investment property. Homes are generally maintained better than investment properties. Sure, the landlord has saved money over the years on maintenance, but the 'saved money' can be wiped off the sale price, and more to boot.

Maintenance along the way makes the investor money in the end.

Save money through maintenance

A small but non-urgent maintenance job, left unattended, can quickly become an expensive issue. If you are vigilant and proactive with maintenance, you will spend a bit more in the beginning, but save a lot more in the end.

It's uncanny how the property manager's and tenant's attitude towards a property often reflects the owner's. If the owner is attentive and responsive to maintenance issues, they will be too. Attention to detail can save investors on many fronts.

But if you have bought a sparkling new unit or house that offers white or light-coloured carpet, non-washable paint and a glass vanity with chippable surfaces, it is unreasonable to expect any tenant to keep it in pristine condition.

Earn money through maintenance

A mistake landlords make with maintenance is to assume the tenants will benefit at the landlord's expense. This is completely false. When a property is well maintained, both landlord and tenant benefit. And the relationship is far more cordial.

Consider the family home and the long-term investment property competing in the market for a tenant. All things being equal in regard to the features of the properties, if a family decide to lease out their treasured (and well-maintained) home for the first time, it will nearly always lease more quickly and for a better price than a pre-existing investment property that has not been maintained.

Well-maintained properties lease more quickly and lease for more. The maintenance earns the landlords more while providing a happier and more responsible tenant.

Prevention is cheaper than cure when it comes to maintenance of investment properties.

<u>53</u> Study no more?

We are all susceptible to marketing. Whether it's fashion, food or houses, to keep the products fresh and appealing there is always a 'must have' on the market. In relation to house appeal for buyers, a trip through the endless array of new display homes will show a pattern of what the sales market thinks we want and will pay for.

Only a few years ago bedrooms were being transformed into home offices and new dwellings had to have one. Study areas were considered important as people began to work longer hours and have fewer children. The advent of the internet also made working from home popular.

Today, because the number of portable electronic devices utilising a wireless internet connection continues to grow, the need for a designated home office is declining. Free access to the internet in cafés, along with wireless hotspotting, has reduced the demand for dial-up and cable connections in the home.

Will this change the way people are connecting to the internet and have an impact on the real estate market? It already has!

Wireless broadband, in combination with laptops, smart phones and iPads, has given people the freedom to work and access the internet away from their home office. In days gone by, people were often either in their home office surfing the internet or downstairs watching television. Now they can do both at once. They watch television while surfing the internet and check social media sites on an iPad or laptop during commercials.

A designated home office or study area holds less importance to a home buyer now, and this subtle change in demand should impact on property values and building trends. Demand for one-bedroom apartments may increase, as will their value, from both a rental and an ownership perspective.

For example, already some medium to large building developments in Sydney's central and inner west are including one- and two-bedroom apartments that do not have designated study areas. As portable electronic communication devices gain an even greater hold, this physical space-saving technology will continue to affect property prices and how properties are presented in a rapidly changing market.

It's not to say that the home office or study area will become extinct or totally irrelevant, but it is one example of how changes in technology can impact on our lifestyle.

Technology impacts on the design features of modern housing.

<u>54</u> Maintaining composure

Good times can breed bad practices. You know the real estate market is strong when buyers submit unconditional contract offers while forgoing due diligence such as building inspections, or when unrenovated properties sell for comparable prices to renovated properties. Such displays of buyer aggression can be explained as 'taking a risk on' trading conditions.

Buyers have a higher appetite for risk when they believe the overall upside in a strong market comfortably outweighs any risk of undetected property defects. While this buyer psychology is common in a buoyant market, that's not to say it is wise behaviour.

In contrast to 'risk on' behaviour, when confidence is slow and prices are stagnant or falling, buyers take a 'risk off' approach to purchases when it is hot.

Many buyers play it too cautiously in soft markets, passing up buying at great value in the process. Anyone who was brave enough to make a purchase in Sydney or Melbourne in 2012 effectively bought at the bottom of the cycle, whether by design or default.

But when the market booms, there is a risk that some buyers may be too aggressive for their own good. Paying for due diligence on multiple properties that you inevitably miss out on can cause you to question the value of doing due diligence. The temptation to pass up on due diligence also increases when reports are written up with multiple disclaimers and cautionary tales that do little to guide you in the right direction.

Getting the all-clear on a pest and building inspection, you can sometimes feel as though the expenditure was wasted. The insurance in ensuring that you have not purchased a problem property makes due diligence the best money you will ever spend.

Even though the information gained from these reports may seem minimal, they can act as safeguards against the discovery of post-purchase structural defects, possibly saving you tens of thousands of dollars later. They are a very worthwhile investment, particularly when their small cost is weighed up against the overall value of the transaction.

There are a few ways to ensure that money is not wasted on due diligence on a property you may not ultimately secure.

Firstly, if the price guide looks too good to be true, it probably is. Everyone is fully aware that bait pricing is rampant. Be pragmatic when assessing what a property is likely to sell for. If it's likely to sell above your budget, don't spend thousands on inspections, strata reports and contracts being read by the lawyer. This is fruitless.

Secondly, ask the owner via the agent or the owner's lawyer what price they would be prepared to sell for today. If you can meet that price, then by all means conduct some due diligence in a rapid timeframe, knowing that it won't be a wasted effort.

Thirdly, see if other buyers have paid for a pest/building inspection. If so, ask if the company that did that report will sell you a copy at a reduced rate or offer a rebate should you miss out on that property. Many companies are happy to do this.

Lastly, don't ignore the obvious. A building inspection report on an unrenovated and unlivable property is going to tell you that the property is unlivable. Don't pretend it's something it's not. If your budget cannot cover a total renovation project, don't engage in one to begin with.

If a property is newly built or just renovated, a building report should still be done prior to purchase. Making a profit from developing is hard work. Disregard what you saw on *The Block*. Many people who attempt to renovate for profit lose money or, at best, merely break even. As this reality starts to dawn, they begin to cut costs to meet their budget. A trained building inspector will pick up on any issues this may cause.

To get full value from a building report or inspector, turn up on site when they are doing the inspection and talk through any practical issues they raise. This often offers more value than just waiting for a written report. Some reports are full of disclaimers and alarmist language, but tell you little about the true state of the home. A conversation with the inspector can add great context and value to the written report.

Strata reports are a great source of information for apartment buyers. Don't just read the minutes of the most recent meeting, but go back several years to ensure there are no festering, unresolved issues. An unexpected special levy shortly after purchasing an apartment for top dollar can set your finances back a long way. If there are any impending levies, they can be factored into your offer or plans.

Paying for due diligence on multiple properties in a competitive market environment can be frustrating, but if you are considering passing up on this pre-purchase research, please note that you may be taking an unjustified risk. The only thing worse than missing out on the right property is buying the wrong one.

Due diligence can mean the difference between buying the right property and buying the wrong one.

<u>55</u> Guidelines and laws to protect home buyers

At last! Across Victoria, NSW and Queensland real estate agents are now more accountable for the price they quote than ever before. Each state government has moved to stamp out the practice known as underquoting or bait pricing.

For years, the preferred trick of many agents was to entice the home seller with the promise of a high price and at the same time lure buyers into bidding with the hope of a low price. The objective was to engineer a sale between the misled parties then blame 'the market' for any discrepancies.

In a soft market, the agent told the seller that 'the market' was to blame for the lower than expected price.

In a strong market, the agent told the aggrieved underbidders that the high price was due to 'the market strength'.

In some instances, property sales will still genuinely exceed expectations, but this will happen less often as a result of the laws introduced during 2015 and 2016.

Updated price guides

In a welcome move, agents must now increase the price guide when or if an offer is made above that guide. In Queensland, the real estate agent cannot give any price guide for a property that is going to public auction.

In most states, it is now law that the agent is forbidden to continue marketing the property at a lower price than has already been offered. This ensures that potential buyers are given an insight into the current price levels at all times of the sales campaign.

These guidelines aimed to protect frustrated and misled underbidders, who were spending thousands of dollars on due diligence. Some buyers may still be frustrated by the true market strength at times, but they are less likely to be blatantly misled by underquoting.

Instances where price guides have been increased mid-campaign to bring them into line with offers and buyer feedback has increased in NSW and Victoria. Only time will tell if this trend continues.

As a result of these guidelines—if they are policed properly—you can expect fewer bidders at each auction. The buyers who cannot win the bidding are priced out of the bidding prior to the auction. A totally fair outcome.

A rising market can see bidding and buyer feedback exceed many agents' price guides very early in their campaigns. Under these circumstances, some agents may have deliberately left prices artificially low to entice more bidders, creating the illusion of frenzy at their auctions.

It has been reported that somewhere between 25 and 30 per cent of all properties scheduled for auction have sold prior to the big day. Given that these guidelines force agents to increase the price guide in line with market feedback, you can expect even more properties to sell prior to auction.

The laws on underquoting in each state are pragmatic, balanced and fair, if they are enforced by relevant government departments. A number of high-profile Melbourne agents were charged with underquoting in late 2016 and early 2017. This will serve as a warning to the industry that Consumer Affairs Victoria (CAV) is serious about stamping out underquoting and bait pricing. The multiple charges against agents highlights how the auction system is highly susceptible to dummy bidders and underquoting.

Buyers (and sellers) should also note the following extract from the NSW Fair Trading Underquoting Property Prices Guidelines:

> When a price range is given, NSW Fair Trading considers the lowest price is the agent's representation to prospective purchasers of a realistic potential selling price.

This particular aspect of the law will protect buyers in a strong market and sellers in a soft market. It's essentially the equivalent of advertising the seller's reserve price. It beggars belief that NSW Fair Trading and Consumer Affairs Victoria (CAV) have had to be so firm in getting agents to tell buyers the price that sellers 'really' want. Given the agents can essentially fudge their paperwork to protect themselves from prosecution, consumers need to remain guarded.

Bidding below the reserve price

In a soft market, agents often promote properties below owners' reserves. When some owners question the merit of such a strategy, their agent assures them that it is simply to create buyer competition and drive the price higher.

The real reason some agents are so determined to promote a property below the seller's reserve price is because they know the reserve is too high, even though it was the agents themselves who originally quoted such a high price. If you think this seems unbelievable conduct in a professional industry, rest assured, many agree with you.

Such tactics don't happen as often in a buoyant market. But when a boom turns into a soft market (which it always does) the guidelines will protect both buyers and sellers.

When looking to buy in a boom market, buyers should accept the market is setting new highs. Under these circumstances, prices will continue to exceed expectations and sales evidence in some instances. Being outbid does not mean the agent has deliberately underquoted. In most instances, it simply means that there was another buyer prepared to bid higher. If you find this unacceptable, then you might do better to wait until the respective boom is over.

When all is said and done, an agent's role is to maximise the selling price for the owner—by fair means. These laws ensure the agent adopts a fair pricing strategy. From there it's up to the open market to decide.

Underquoting laws make agents more accountable for the prices they quote to home buyers.

<u>56</u> How to bid, buy and win at auction

Now we have canvassed the tricks and traps inherent in home buying, and the due diligence that should always apply, it is time to face the stressful, and for many quite scary, prospect of having to take part in an auction. Even if you are fiercely determined to avoid being caught up in an auction when buying, it could come down to that to secure your dream home.

There are plenty of anecdotes about people walking away shattered 'because someone else always seems to win'. That's because most people attend auctions without a bidding strategy. The good news is you may win an auction without having reached your predetermined maximum price. The bad news is you may be the underbidder at a few auctions before you come out on top.

An understanding of bidding strategies provides you with an advantage that can save you many thousands of dollars and give you the best chance of auction success.

Patrick Bright is one of the original buyer's agents in the Sydney property market. Bright has bid at more auctions than most people have attended in a lifetime. He is also a former selling agent and licensed auctioneer. His experience offers invaluable insights into the stakes at play and how best to manage the auction, the auctioneer and competing bidders.

Bright reports that there has been a noticeable increase in the number of buyers employing someone to bid at auction on their behalf. As vendors employ a selling agent to maximise their price, he explains, buyers are 'hiring someone of equal knowledge and skill to save them money when buying'.

Bright encourages those who believe registered bidding has killed off the 'dreaded dummy bidder' to think again. From experience, he believes that dummy bidders are still very much a part of many auctions. Dummy bidders could conceivably be placed by either vendor or agent, though Bright believes few sales agents would take such a risk.

Auctions need competitive bidding. For the vendor, it's a simple task to have a friend register and bid up to the reserve price to create the illusion that the property is in demand.

How do you hold an auction with only one buyer? This is when an agent underquotes the price to attract more bidders. According to Bright and others in the industry, you may also be bidding against a dummy bidder, placed by the owner or agent!

Auctions are fluid and unpredictable events. The simple advice for buyers is to avoid bidding unless the property has met or exceeded reserve. In the past, less skilled auctioneers would call the property on the market as soon as it hit reserve.

Skilled auctioneers won't immediately advise the crowd when the reserve has been met. If the auction is doing well, Bright says, the auctioneer won't want to give bidders a sense the auction has just reached the vendor's walk-away price.

A good, assertive bidder will have no qualms about asking the auctioneer if the property is 'on the market yet'. You may or may not get an answer to that question, but it is worth asking, and continuing to ask during the auction.

Put simply, there are two types of auctions:

- auctions where the pressure is on the buyers due to buyer competition
- auctions where the pressure is on the vendor due to insufficient competition above the reserve.

To adopt the right strategy, you first need to get a handle on which category the auction you are bidding at falls into.

Outbidding the competition

If there are more than five or six genuine bidders at the auction, either it is an attractive property or the agent has underquoted the price. Remain calm in the face of multiple bidders. Many are there looking for a bargain, because that's what the agent's price guide suggested was on offer.

To flush out the serious buyers, Bright suggests that one strategy you can employ is to bid early and relatively close to fair value. He recounts a story about how his first bid on a property with a price guide of $850 000 was $1 million.

'Many of the underbidders were misled into being there on the day and I just wanted to knock them out early and send a message to those who were left.' The selling agent admitted to Bright that he made him 'look bad in front of the underbidders' because his opening bid was so strong. When you know the fair value is $1 million and beyond, why waste time bidding at $800 000? You put yourself in a far stronger position by bidding decisively and early as a means of dictating terms.

If you are in an auction with intense buyer competition, Bright advises bidding assertively, quickly and confidently. By starting strongly, you rob the seller's agent and the auctioneer of the spectacle. While Bright may win only 20 to 30 per cent of the auctions he bids at on behalf of clients, he always bids confidently up to the agreed maximum price. You need to be equally confident with your last bid as you were with your first.

The reality is that inexperienced bidders are easily intimidated in the auction environment. It is almost a cliché that underbidders will remark, 'We knew the other guy was going to keep bidding, so we just stopped.' You can use that fear to your advantage. If you can bluff the competition into ceasing to bid against you, the amount saved becomes a saving for you and a loss for the vendor. It happens all the time at auctions.

'Project confidence down to your last bid, and never look as though you are near your limit,' Bright recommends. 'Spook underbidders with the ferocity of your bidding, because people don't want to bid against a crazy.'

Take up a position where you can see the entire field of bidders, and look for signs of distress among your competition. If this sounds savage and unnecessarily confrontational, welcome to the auction system. Remember, as a buyer you are only responding to the vendor's selected sale process.

Bright insists that every client provide him with a written maximum price prior to the auction. He refuses to speak to his client during the auction and does not allow a client to increase their maximum once the auction has started. 'We have the tough conversation about price before the auction begins.' The property's value has been researched and the buyer's finance has been approved. A buyer can't get caught up in the drama of the auction.

The question bidders ultimately need to ask themselves before an auction is, 'What is our walk-away price for this property?' No matter how special a property may be, every buyer has a walk-away price. Whether it is governed by common sense, good judgement or finance restrictions, you need to establish your walk-away price before the auction.

Enter every auction knowing you may not win it. An auction should only be won on the right price and terms.

Even in a strong market, about one-third of sales are above market price, one-third are at market value and the balance are sales where the vendor drops their price on the day to get a sale.

Given that about one in three auctions will sell above market price, you need to be clear on your predetermined limit before the auction. Just because you set a predetermined limit above fair market price, it does not mean you will necessarily be called on to pay that amount.

In 20 years, Bright says, he has never reached his authorised maximum on the auctions he has won. 'The only time I reach the client's maximum price is at the auctions I lose. So I inform clients upfront "you will likely kiss a few frogs before you win one" when it comes to auctions. The auction you win will be won below your maximum bid, because the only people who reach their maximum at an auction are the underbidders.'

Gavin Norris, the CEO of Chinese real estate website Juwai, was interviewed in August 2016 about Chinese bidding tactics at auctions. Norris noted the high sophistication of Chinese buyers at auctions. 'It's not because they overpay—it's because, like every smart buyer, they fight for every dollar. If a Chinese buyer doesn't feel comfortable at auctions...they...ask a friend...to stand in for them.' Norris relates that this ensures the bidding is being conducted by someone cool headed and more experienced with the auction process.

In the same article, auctioneer James Pratt offered buyers this advice: 'Don't be afraid to slow the auction down or to bid in uneven increments.' Buyers have become more comfortable with the auction process and are more likely to assert themselves rather than following the auctioneer's instructions.

Bidding and buying at a slow auction

Fortunately, not every auction you bid at will be vigorous. Even though the vendor has been told an auction will put pressure on the buyers, the pressure often rests with the vendor.

A slow auction can be an excruciating and agonising event to witness. The vendor has gone to auction with visions of five bidders trying to knock each other out with a big cheque. The buyer's belief and resolve that the owner wants too much is hardened when they see a lack of buyer competition.

A slow auction with only one or two registered bidders is more like watching a negotiation than a competitive auction.

When an auction is struggling to get started, Bright's preference is to place a bid as opposed to seeing the auction pass in. If the auction passes in, the owner's resolve around their reserve price tends to firm up. Remember that while the auction is still alive, the owners are more likely to make a price concession under pressure to gain a sale.

Once the auction has finished and the crowd has left, the pent-up pressure the owners have been feeling dissipates.

If you make a bid, even if it is below the owner's reserve, you are likely to elicit a counterbid from the auctioneer and/or the vendor. This counter-bid is usually in the form of a 'vendor's bid'. Such a bid will give a good insight into the vendor's price expectations. Where the vendor's bid is in relation to yours will govern whether you strike a deal or walk away.

A lot of buyers actually reduce their predetermined limit mid-auction in a slow market or at a slow auction. They go to the auction prepared to pay $1 million, but watch the competition drop out at $930 000. Suddenly, $950 000 seems like a fair offer in the buyer's mind. Why would we pay $1 million when everyone else has dropped out at $930 000, they reason?

In a slow auction, the agent has a lot of work to do to get the sale together. At a strong auction with multiple bidders above the reserve, the agent can afford simply to watch proceedings without needing to have any heavy conversations with their vendor. This luxury does not exist if all the bidding is below the reserve price.

If the auction is struggling and you are the highest bidder, ask the agent to disclose the reserve price to you, so you can make a decision on it. By doing so you will gain a specific figure that will buy the property at that moment in time.

If the bidding stalls below the reserve and the owner won't drop their reserve to 'meet the market', then it may be best to move on to another opportunity in the market. The good news is you won't have to pressure the owner to drop their price. The agent is likely to be employing every conditioning and crunching tactic they know to get the vendor down in price.

Remember, the objective is to buy a good property at a fair price. If you attempt to steal the property for a bargain price, the vendor is likely to relist on the market as a private treaty.

It is reasonable to aim to work the vendor down from an above-market price reserve to a market-based reserve. If you attempt to work the price down from a reserve price to a bargain level, another buyer is highly likely to come in over the top of you.

Auctioneer James Pratt and buyer's agent Patrick Bright agree on one thing. If the property is going to be passed in, be sure to make the last, highest bid. This ensures you have the first right to negotiate with the seller once the auction has failed.

In-room versus onsite auctions

Auctions will be held onsite at the subject property or offsite, at what is commonly referred to as in-room auctions. There are no fundamental differences in how they both work, but some subtle ways in which they operate may be worth keeping an eye on.

At an onsite auction, while you may be greeted by a massive crowd, it's worth remembering that most of them are neighbours, not bidders. Also, at an onsite auction, if you stand in the right position, you should be able to view all the competing bidders.

Many experienced bidders like to stand close to the auctioneer and look at the crowd from that vantage point. Such brazen confidence from a bidder can be unnerving to other bidders.

Patrick Bright believes an onsite auction can be more emotional than an in-room auction. 'Given the buyers are actually standing in the house they are bidding on, it can play to the vendor's advantage. Conversely, a rainy day, aircraft noise or excessive car traffic can have a negative impact on an onsite auction, while these issues are irrelevant with in-room auctions,' he says.

Bright points out that the order of the properties to be auctioned at in-room auctions is highly relevant. From his experience, properties certain to sell well will be auctioned first. The agents are aiming to create a 'positive tone' to the proceedings. They will also want to place a certain seller last in the pecking order to ensure that the event both starts and finishes well. The weaker auctions are likely to be buried in the middle of the schedule.

With so many bidders for a range of different properties at an in-room auction, it's much more difficult to know who you are bidding against.

Power at an auction is fluid, flowing back and forth between the vendor and the buyers. The more buyers there are, the more power the vendor has, and vice versa.

If buying at auction is daunting for you, consider outsourcing the bidding or making your best offer prior to auction. Just because the agent wants the vendor to go to auction, it does not mean you have to buy that way.

Always have a bidding strategy before you go to a property auction. A live auction is a tough place for an emotional home buyer to learn the game.

<u>57</u> Why invest in property?

If the old saying 'love where you live' applies to home buying, then a dramatically less emotional equation should come into play when considering an investment property. This is a business proposition and, as such, needs to be viewed in an entirely different way from how you would approach buying your own home.

While all the basic rules of due diligence and seeking the best value for money in a sound property apply, you need to take off the rose-coloured glasses you might wear when out home hunting.

Many investors, particularly the so-called mum-and-dad variety, may be tempted by those seminars promising to 'make you rich from property'. That claim should ring the first alarm bell. As a novice, you are captive to someone else's 'guide book' on how easy it all is, with plenty of examples of happy outcomes thrown in as bait.

Let's work from the outset on the basis that if something seems too good to be true, then the safest bet is to assume that it probably is. Add to this the fact that it involves a large outlay, probably using equity in an existing property to stake the first purchase, and the amateur investor can rapidly accrue unserviceable debt.

It cannot be said too often that emotion has no place in this type of property dealing. It should be viewed from beginning to end purely as a business proposition; otherwise, welcome to the predatory world of investment 'educators' and 'gurus'.

There are as many traps for the uninformed in this arena as there are in any other type of property purchase. By understanding the basic principles employed by seasoned and successful investors, you can carry out some well-informed research and avoid much of the 'hard sell' that surrounds this area. Anything that needs to be 'hard sold' should always be treated with great caution.

Armed with the right checklist, you can decide to move forward with a sensible and achievable outcome in mind, or think again whether property investment best suits your resources and needs.

You may be convinced that any property that can be rented is a good bet, that you can get great tax deductions along the way, and that you can then either sell it for a profit or turn it into a positive income stream as part of a retirement package. And this may indeed be achievable, but only if you get all the elements right.

Seasoned investors follow a specific set of rules. The first reality check is to understand that this is not a short-term proposition. Unlike other investment vehicles, such as shares, there is no quick divesting if it turns a little sour, or even if it shows a good return. It's essential to get the financial and buying formula right to begin with. Investors must factor in all the add-on costs just to buy a property, the lead times to settlement without income from tenants, and the fact that any bailout is not just a phone call away.

Many still see negative gearing as the way for mum-and-dad investors to enter this market, but there is a high level of vulnerability and misinformation involved here. A wide range of variables come into play, not least of which is ensuring you fully understand the type of debt-fuelled equations that usually apply.

The first lesson revolves around what 'unemotional' buying means. When we set out to buy a home that we plan to live in and love, we see things very differently. Imagine the furniture and décor, the sought-after dream kitchen, the potential for an extension to create more space, applying our own colour palette and window furnishings, and all our plans for the outdoor areas. Few people methodically add up what they spend to make their home into their personally tailored nest, and for a very good reason. We don't generally regard our primary place of residence purely as a hard-headed investment. We live in it, love it, and adapt it to our personal needs and comfort.

It stands to reason that well-located, established properties in good, livable condition are likely to show the most consistent growth over the long term. Investment property needs to follow the same general rules. Whether it's an apartment, unit development or free-standing property, a lot will depend on your finances and staying power.

What you are fundamentally looking for are clean, easily maintained, well-located properties in sound condition that offer consistent rental income, whatever the wider market may be doing.

The overused term 'well-located' can be a trap for the unwary investor. Close to a city centre or in a buoyant economic zone, with lots of public transport, parking and amenities, is one thing. Niche locations are quite another.

Many tales of woe have been told by first-time investors who have mistaken holiday properties for investment opportunities. You get to use it for a beach or ski holiday and at other times rent it out for an inflated amount. The trouble is, the time you want it is when most others do too. Seasonal rentals often mean a high level of wear and tear, and long periods of vacancy during the rest of the year. When the season shuts down, so too does demand, especially as many of these locations don't have large permanent populations.

Common traps include buying generic apartments in high-risk, high-rise locations, where the chances of capital gain are likely to be low; failing to take into account the types of amenities likely to attract long-term tenants; and finding your hand is constantly in your pocket to cover unforeseen repairs.

With the right business approach and market knowledge, investment property can be successful.

58 Debt and equity

For potential property investors, the first and most important research should be how to finance such an investment. Too many people leave it to the 'investment experts'. If you sign up to attend a property investors' course, expect to hear a lot about equity and valuations. That boils down to how to use the equity you have in an existing property—usually your home—and how the increase in value of the investment property will create its own equity. The idea is that as soon as the value increases, you use the equity to acquire another investment property.

Equity is the paper value of the property you own after costs against the asset (mortgage) are deducted. When the market rises your equity increases, and when it falls the equity decreases.

But you would be better advised to focus on debt and equity. Equity and valuations fluctuate with the market. Other than the money you pay towards the principal of the loan, debt will remain, regardless of market conditions.

When the market rises, debt becomes a decreasing percentage of the property. Your equity and valuation increase too. That's the good news and the only good news you are likely to hear at many investment seminars.

When the market falls, though, debt becomes a bigger percentage of the property. Be wary of anyone who peddles the notion that real estate prices do not fall. Real estate falls everywhere at some time. The size of the correction may vary, but all markets correct eventually.

Accepting that real estate tends to rise over the long term is completely different from claiming real estate never falls in price.

Most investment course content can be summarised in three words: debt, valuation and equity. For example:

- Buy a property with minimum money down and maximum *debt*, wait for it to rise in value or do some minor renovations to increase the value.

- Get a *valuation* for the highest price you can, thereby creating equity on paper.

- Buy another property using the *equity* you gained on the previous property.

- Repeat process.

You will see this process promoted as a means by which 'everyday folk' can acquire and 'own' 20 or 30 properties in just four years! But it would be just as accurate to say that they have taken on the risk and debt levels of 20 to 30 properties, given the debt-fuelled strategy that has been adopted.

In fairness, this strategy would have worked well in Sydney and Melbourne during the boom period of 2012–2016. But it is crucial to recognise that Sydney experienced a generational boom. These market conditions were not normal trading conditions. It remains to be seen if Sydney is able to maintain these price levels over the next five years, particularly if we move to more normal interest rate settings.

Be warned: if the market drops, those who have adopted the debt, valuation and equity system will have declining equity and rising debt.

Remember, everyone is a genius at the end of a boom. Only the savvy look smart at the start of a correction. If you are the one who arrives late to the party and the market drops shortly after you purchase, you will be staring at negative equity.

Investors who are negatively geared also have to find the money to top up the mortgage repayments.

The best protection against debt is to manage your debt responsibly. When rental income covers both running costs and mortgage repayments, a market downturn won't hurt you very much. You may not 'own 20 properties', but you will be structured to prosper in good times as well as in bad. You will be protected against stormy weather.

Equity fluctuates with the market. Debt is consistent regardless of market conditions. Remain aware of your debt-to-equity ratio at all times.

<u>59</u> Vacancy

If there is one factor than can be said to be the investor's enemy, it is vacancy. More than half of all property investors' budgets rely on income for 52 weeks of the year. The reality is that less than half of all investment properties generate that amount in any given year. Vacancy is an unwelcome reality of being a property investor. Along with maintenance neglect, vacancy can be cruel to the investor's income return.

Lost income is like lost sleep—you can never make it up. It's gone. While it's impossible to avoid vacancy, there are several crucial decisions you can make to ensure increased occupancy.

Fair market rent

If you always aim to get the absolute top dollar or above market rent, you may well succeed at times. It's on the occasions when your property sits vacant because it is overpriced that a lot of income can be lost. Pricing a $500/week property above the market by $30 a week means that after just three weeks of vacancy you essentially come out even—that is, if you find a tenant at the inflated figure after three weeks, which you probably won't. If you display stubbornness and stay overpriced (and vacant) beyond the three-week mark, you are going backwards at the rate of $500 a week in an attempt to make $30 more a week. It's easy to fall into this game of pride, but it's nearly impossible to beat the market consistently.

The market is the market. The market price is the price at which people want to lease your property. Above-market price is the price at which no one wants to lease your property, because it's priced too high in comparison to other properties on the market. If your property is marketed correctly and there are no takers, it's probably overpriced.

The market won't always rise. It won't always be where you want it to be. That's how markets are. If you are always prepared to accept fair market rent, you will greatly minimise vacancy. The rental markets in most capital cities have rewarded landlords with consistent growth. To capture that growth, just ensure that rent reviews by the managing agent are timely and market-based.

Rent reviews/renewals

The same principle should apply to rent reviews as applies to pricing a property at fair market rent. Turnover of tenants always leads to a vacancy period. It's best to keep a good paying, fair-priced tenant in place, rather than lose them because you overreached in the rent review. The beauty of rent renewals is you avoid added letting fees and there is no break in income generated by the property.

Lease expirations

There are times during the year when properties lease well and times when they don't. The depths of winter and December are traditionally awkward times of year to find tenants in most major markets. Conversely, the beginning of the year is always very robust and active, as people set themselves up for the forthcoming year, perhaps after changing jobs and locations.

So it's best to ensure the lease expiration date avoids these awkward leasing periods.

Lease periods are negotiable; they don't necessarily have to be six or 12 months. If a six-month lease is due to expire on December 15, insist on making it a seven-month lease, expiring on January 15 the following year. That way, if the tenant decides to leave on expiration of the lease, you have a vacant property at a prime leasing time. Focusing on the lease expiration date can easily save unnecessary vacancy.

Property profile

Certain properties are prone to regular tenant turnover. While the return looks good on paper when you are buying it, that strong yield will apply only if it's leased 52 weeks a year. A property that is vacant twice a year will likely generate income for only about 48 weeks a year, with the landlord paying double the letting fees to boot. Before purchasing an investment property, talk to an experienced local property manager about the types of dwellings that lease best and turn over least.

Tenant profile

Good tenant selection will greatly aid your quest to minimise vacancy. A letting agent will do the tenant assessments and recommend the best fit for your property. That's in the ideal world, where there is a wide selection of eager tenants to choose from. You are paying the agent a monthly fee to manage the property and handle all the direct tenant contact. It is usually preferable that the tenant never knows who the property owner is. This is a business arrangement.

When the letting agent recommends a new tenant, take a purely business approach to the suitability of the prospective tenant. Bear in mind that often the agent would far prefer to see their management fees rolling in than have prospective tenants knocked back. The 'oversell' in this area can be as hyped up as in any other property sector.

'Have we found the ideal tenant for you!' may sound persuasive coming from a rental agent. If you feel squeamish about examining that 'ideal tenant' in detail, then think again. It is not a question of discriminating against individuals, but rather of not forcing square pegs into round holes. As an extreme example, a family of five in a two-bedroom apartment is only going to end one way. Share house arrangements can turn into conflicts that leave you holding a vacant 'baby'. Determine and then stick to what type of tenancy suits your property and benefits both parties.

Rejecting tenants who are not suited to your property may create an unwelcome vacancy period in the beginning, but it will save you a great deal of pain and lost income in the future. The longer you own the investment, the more adept you will become at identifying the right tenant profile.

* * *

The first rule for investors is 'Don't lose money'. Unnecessary and avoidable vacancy is lost income and lost income should never be dismissed as tax deductible or insignificant. As the old saying goes, 'Look after the pennies, and the pounds will take care of themselves.'

Work to minimise vacancy periods, and the lost income they cause, through pragmatic tenant selection.

<u>60</u> Five questions for investors

If you are a potential investor, answering the following basic questions before making any buying decisions can help you avoid some of the many pitfalls of the property market. People are attracted to this form of investment—as opposed to shares or shorter-term options, for example—for different reasons. Be clear about what you are basing your overall decision on before buying an investment property. As one seasoned property player observed, you won't get rich quickly with property investment but you can go broke quickly.

1. What is the *net* yield?

Frighteningly, many residential investors don't know how to calculate net yield on their investment. They see a black-and-white equation where, for example, a property is leasing for $1000 a week, and they do their modelling around a $52 000 a year income. The only figure that counts for investors is the amount left over after all costs have been covered. Strata scheme fees, council rates, water rates, land tax, vacancy, agents' fees and maintenance are costs that can take 20 to 30 per cent off the gross yield. The $52 000 you thought you were getting just turned into $36 400.

2. Are you chasing *yield* or *capital growth*?

In the search for growth, many investors disregard the importance of a strong yield supporting the investment. The best investment properties provide good yields that continue to appreciate. The predictable and growing yield ensures that capital growth follows. A property with a weak return, tipping you into negative gearing, then needs to experience strong capital growth just to offset the negative gearing. Buying on the basis that a property has sound income fundamentals is investing. Buying on the basis that hopefully someone in the future will pay a higher price than you just paid is speculating.

3. Is the investment decision *tax based* or *performance based?*

If you ask your accountant how to save tax through negative gearing, they will certainly be able to help. A good tax-saving property can be a dud investment, though. The goal when investing is to profit. Negative gearing is a fancy term for weekly loss. Many investors sell out of positively geared properties because the property is creating a 'tax problem'. If you are paying tax, you are profiting. If negatively geared, you are losing. Even though the taxman splits the loss with you, half a loss is still a loss. Buy good real estate and capital growth and yield growth will come.

As a wise man once said, 'You are better off sharing a profit with the taxman than keeping a loss to yourself.'

4. Where do you think we are in the *current cycle?*

This applies to the market at the time you are considering buying. It may be that rents are down while property prices are rising; interest rates may go down further and the market may appear to have its mojo back in some major capital city locations. Credible forecasters and economists contradict each other daily on what will happen with the property market going forward. Listen to all the key messages then form your own view before purchasing an investment property.

Many people want to get rich quick in property. More people have 'gone broke quick' by trying to do so, so be careful in your ambitions. It can't be said often enough that property investment is not a quick fix or a short-term proposition. Take a long view (10-plus years) on quality property and you should do well. If you take a punt on a quick profit in the market, then understand the risk you are running.

5. Are you location-centric in your outlook?

Residential property investors have a tendency to invest close to home. Often it is fear of the unknown and a lack of knowledge about other markets that steer people closer to home, towards the more familiar.

But there are opportunities out there for those prepared to look. Take what we call 'Cinderella suburbs', for instance. They often border high-growth areas and show signs of increasing demand as buyers are pushed out of the more expensive neighbouring suburbs. In time, a Cinderella suburb will turn into a princess for the patient investor. Many in the property market refer to this phenomenon as the 'ripple effect'.

The best investment buying in the residential sector may well be in capital cities outside of the one you live in. Again, unfamiliar territory, but research and follow where the trends may be heading. For example, in the 12 months to February 2017, Hobart was one of the best places to have invested in Australia. This result may be surprising for many, but astute investors in the market profited handsomely on Hobart property.

It's not a case of 'anything will do', either. Buying outside of your known territory requires an understanding of which areas in an unfamiliar territory are likely to show the best growth.

Coupled with that is an understanding of what underpins the economy of a certain location. Houses in mining towns in Western Australia have lost 50 to 80 per cent of their value, taking property investors down too. If the local economy is a one-trick pony based on a specific industry sector for growth and survival, then investing there is tantamount to gambling. Unfortunately, many people think they are investing when they are actually gambling. If the demand and jobs of today turn into a serious downturn tomorrow, then circumstances beyond your control have left you with a stranded asset as the tenants leave town.

We saw Perth undergo a major correction as the resources boom wound back. Many investors who entered that market bought at a high price because they anticipated ongoing demand. Many were left floundering when it came time to sell. Tomorrow does come in these situations.

Your investment decision should be driven by fundamentals that promise growth, not geographical convenience.

The transaction

<u>61</u> Beating remorse

Buying real estate is the most significant purchase many people make in their lives. It can take months to find your dream home. If you stay at it long enough, though, you will find it! Then at last the grind of giving up weekends and traipsing around inspections is over.

But at this point many people experience conflicting emotions. They are excited, but also fearful. Nagging little questions pop up that won't go away. Are we making a mistake? Is the price right? Can we afford it? Is it a good neighbourhood? Such questions can cast a pall of doubt over what seemed like an obvious decision.

It is normal to begin questioning the wisdom of the purchase either just before or immediately after signing the contracts. A lot of people go through this emotion—it is called buyer's remorse. And it can cross a wide range of situations. Going through the normal jitters after what you considered to be a well-researched and doggedly pursued goal is one thing. Having made an overexcited, spontaneous, impulsive purchase of something as significant as a property is another. The reasons for those doubts are also many and varied.

But the best way to handle this is to acknowledge it when it arises. Maybe you are certain the property is the right one, but your partner has grave reservations. Meet buyer's remorse head on.

Psychologists say we buy emotionally and then justify with logic. Buyer's remorse is your mind at work looking to justify the purchase logically. If you ignore the questions that pop up, they will simply keep coming back and will potentially escalate into a much bigger problem.

Write down your major concerns or questions as a list of pros and cons. What specific issues have caused negative thoughts to creep in? This will help greatly in identifying the real issues causing concern. Balance that with the positives and what ticks the right boxes that swayed you towards this property to begin with. You can then consider specifics, as opposed to questioning anything and everything perceived as negative to do with the purchase. Some of those negatives may well turn into manageable positives instead.

The main consideration, though, is to avoid rash decisions if you are experiencing buyer's remorse. If you have not signed the contract, delay doing so by a day or two while you take a rational look at the concerns. Any desire to pull out today may be replaced by a determination to finalise the purchase tomorrow. On the other hand, the desire to buy today may be replaced by a determination to rescind tomorrow.

Settling on whether to proceed or to pull out will be a decision you make at your own pace, based on logic.

Meet buyer's remorse head on and address any regrets logically rather than emotionally. Write concerns down and they tend to diminish.

<u>62</u> What should we offer?

Having finally found a suitable home, there is a new challenge. What to offer the vendor? There are so many variables when it comes to making an offer that you are entitled to feel confused. Put simply, there are more questions than answers once you find a property that meets your needs.

Do you present a one-off best offer, with a take-it-or-leave-it attitude? Or perhaps it's a case of starting low and working up to your maximum price? Maybe wait for the auction? Once you make an offer, how long do you leave it on the table?

The questions keep coming as you ponder how to secure your dream home. When purchasing an investment property, you are more emotionally detached, but the home buyers you are bidding against may be emotionally engaged. Setting a game plan is the key to success when making an offer.

If you have found a home you are unable to let go, there is the risk of being left devastated if you miss out, or of overpaying to secure it. It's okay to overpay to secure a desired property, as long as you know you are overpaying and can afford to do so (though this is less true for investors). Many people who 'overpaid' 10 years ago now look back on the purchase as a bargain.

Three prices

If your focus is on the competition when buying, then prepare to be drawn into the game. Whether at the auction or in trading information through the selling agent, understand that games will be played. If you focus on what other buyers are prepared to pay when determining your offer, then the desire to purchase the property can be hijacked by a complete stranger's interpretation of value.

Buyers who focus completely on the competition end up dazed and confused. The key is to work out, not what the property is worth to the competing buyer, but rather what it is worth to you.

The best way to enter a negotiation for a property purchase is to accept that there are three prices: good value, fair market price and expensive. A full awareness of the three prices for every property can act as your guide through the negotiations.

Good value

Not many homes have sold for what could be termed good value in recent times. Sometimes the market has been rising so quickly that expensive on the day of exchange is good value at settlement. In a falling market, the opposite is true. A purchase that seems good value when contracts are exchanged looks expensive by the time the buyer collects the keys at settlement.

Aside from abnormally sharp movements in the market, you can only ever transact on the available information. Whether you are buying or selling, it's best for your sanity not to study the market once you have transacted. It won't change anything.

Many buyers love to claim they achieved good value—a bargain. In reality, only about 10 per cent of all transactions fit into the good value category. Good value is any property that sells for below market price. The value left on the table may be due to a desperate vendor, a poorly run sales campaign or a hidden feature that everyone except the buyer missed (such as development potential).

Even if you find a grossly incompetent agent who compromises the vendor's position, it's worth noting that you are still negotiating with a vendor who wants fair market price for their asset. Buyers who prey on weak agents with weak vendors carry bad karma.

Everyone loves to criticise the stock trader who offers unsuspecting people below market price for their shares, in the hope they won't know the value of them. The real estate market is full of people with the same mindset that our dubious stockbroker displays to the vulnerable in the share market.

If you are aiming to purchase below market value, be sure you don't buy a compromised or flawed property thinking you have nabbed a bargain. This is more common than buyers who successfully buy a bargain.

One of the most common sources of good value is stale properties that were initially overpriced. These properties continue to languish even once they are priced correctly. They often need to be priced below market value to ignite interest. If you do find a home that is languishing on the market, judge it on the price, not on the length of the selling campaign.

Fair market price

Agents claim they got $200 000 over reserve and the buyers claim they got a bargain. So what really happened? It probably sold for fair market price. With a 5 per cent variance, most transactions occur at fair market price. Buyers who are prepared to pay a fair market price will always end up securing a home, unless they are buying in a rapidly rising market. That's not to say they will always secure the home they really want, though. Murphy's Law states that if you really want a particular home at fair market price, others will too.

Expensive

Intense buyer competition is what usually causes properties to sell above the market price. Even though the home is desirable, the recent sales evidence of similar homes does not support the sale price. Buyer emotion took it past fair market price, making it an expensive purchase.

* * *

When interviewed after an auction, agents often claim to have beaten the market by the inflated amount. The reality is they quoted below market price and sold for fair market price, creating an illusion of the sale being stronger than it really was. That's not to say that there are not outstanding results being produced by real estate agents, but it takes a savvy market watcher to distinguish between agent spin and reality.

If you are buying real estate, you owe it to yourself to pragmatically establish the three prices for your target property before commencing negotiations. Doing so will help you accept the outcome, whether or not you are successful.

Identifying the three prices of your target property will put you in a stronger buying position.

63 Why the price guide is no guide at all

Interpreting agents' price guides has become harder for many home buyers than earning enough money to purchase a property. Each agency takes a different tack on how to position their listings to the market.

Some firms price accurately; some advertise artificially low prices well below market price, in an attempt to bait price buyers along to the auction; others price high, hoping to give their client (seller) room to negotiate down.

One of the greatest errors a buyer can make is to submit an offer based solely on the agent's price guide, or to assume the true value of the property is even loosely related to that agent's guide. As many will attest, these are sad but true facts about buying.

Buyers have learned the hard way that it's common for properties to sell for more than 30 per cent above the agent's price guide.

Those who are conditioned to this style of selling can fall into the trap of adding 20 to 30 per cent to every agent's price guide. In the process, they are unintentionally ruling themselves out of the running for homes that are priced accurately and are affordable.

The frustration doubles when a suitable property sells within your price guide that you did not even bid on, thinking it was going to sell 'way over'.

The rule with price guides is simple: believe nothing and check everything.

Attend inspections and auctions of every home in the immediate area you are interested in. Become an expert on the market, then form a clear view of what your target property is worth and what you are prepared to pay for it.

There is nothing wrong with assessing the value of your dream home and being prepared to pay slightly over the odds to secure it. (Remember that this is not a great strategy for investors, though.) Slightly overpaying to secure your dream home is fine. But being misled, week in week out, by agents who are simply lying is demoralising.

If the agent's price guide seems too low, it probably is. If it seems too high, it probably is.

When a consumers' affairs department claims they cannot find evidence of underquoting, take note that they are simply looking in the wrong place.

The price guide is often no guide at all.

Research the value of your target property independently of the agent's price guide.

<u>64</u> Bracket creep

Buyers are paying higher prices for property, and more stamp duty too. That's great for state government coffers, but not so good for buyers when there's an extra lump attached to already considerable buy-in costs.

The only thing worse than knowing you have a big bill to pay is not knowing about it. This would sum up how the stamp duty bill applies to many home buyers. They know stamp duty exists and it's going to be large, but they still get a shock when the time to pay arrives.

One of the main reasons stamp duty gives so many buyers bill shock is because the amount payable accelerates as prices rise. This sliding scale varies from state to state.

In NSW, at a purchase price of $400 000, the stamp duty payable by a home buyer is $13 490 or 3.37 per cent. At $1 million, the stamp duty is $40 490 or 4.05 per cent. At $2 million, the stamp duty is a whopping $95 490 or 4.77 per cent. The percentage of stamp duty payable increases as you go higher in price.

In South Australia, the stamp duty payable on $1 million is $48 830.

In time, inflation and price rises will mean stamp duty will be nudging 5.5 per cent unless this bracket creep is addressed. At this point, that seems improbable. But most of Sydney's inner ring suburbs, and many in Melbourne, now have a median price well in excess of $1 million. That too seemed highly improbable not so long ago.

As the inner west housing market of Sydney surged by 20 per cent, stamp duty rose by an even greater percentage due to the acceleration in the formula used to calculate it. For full and specific details in your state or territory, go to the relevant government website to ascertain the stamp duty payable on your purchase. Do so before buying.

When you are buying in a boom, a 5 per cent tax on top of the purchase price is not to be dismissed lightly. If for some unforeseen reason you need to resell, once all the other purchasing and selling costs are factored in, it essentially means the property needs to rise 10 per cent before you break even.

While a new car drops 10 per cent of its value when you drive it out of the lot, the new house owes you 10 per cent when you unlock the front door for the first time.

The reality is that state governments are highly unlikely to offer buyers relief on stamp duty. Stamp duty is a major contributor to their overall budgets. Unfortunately, you can't avoid stamp duty. You can only budget for it.

To avoid bill shock, always calculate the exact amount of stamp duty payable in addition to the price you offer the vendor. Do this before making an offer to ensure your financial modelling holds up. While the vendor does not get the 4 or 5 per cent you pay in stamp duty, it still has to be paid.

Calculate the stamp duty payable on your purchase **before** *buying to avoid bill shock.*

<u>65</u> Trading space for location

There is now another player emerging in the quest for apartments, townhouses and smaller properties closer to our major capital cities. Baby boomers competing with first-home buyers and investors for that all-important locational advantage are increasingly being joined in the race by young families.

As traffic continues to clog the roads of our major capital cities, young families are opting to sacrifice space to stay closer to the CBD. Apartments and townhouses that were once considered unsuitable for families are now in demand. Aside from being well located, inner-city strata title properties tend to be similar in price to (if not cheaper than) larger houses in the suburbs.

Smaller terraces and semis without large backyards are also in high demand by young families. As a result, local parks have enjoyed a resurgence in popularity. Local councils do terrific work upgrading and improving local parks, which has made the adjustment to smaller dwellings easier for young families.

Internationally, apartment living for families is not a new concept; for many in other countries it is the norm. It still goes slightly against the grain in the context of the long-held Australian dream of a free-standing home on a quarter-acre block, but the reality has shifted. Indeed, buying into an apartment as a stepping-stone towards eventually buying a house is a logical path.

Sydney's inner west has been at the forefront as lifestyle preferences have changed. The reality is that Sydney living has become more and more difficult to navigate. Jumping in the car and heading across town is an ordeal if travelling at a busy time. And where that busy time was once considered the typical peak hour to and from work, now there is not much difference between weekday and weekend traffic flows (jams).

The impact of work travel and lifestyle on the property market can't be overestimated. The bonus for those seeking such an option comes in proximity to reliable public transport. Recent research suggests that rent growth for properties served by new infrastructure such as the inner west light rail line in Sydney have outperformed the broader market. That 'close to public transport' tag has long been a valuable factor and the widening of the buyer pool creates even greater demand for this. Investors take note!

With investors, first-home buyers and baby boomers being natural purchasers of such apartment stock, along with more young families now considering apartment living, the demand may well be there to meet the ever-increasing supply. This will be a positive for the overall market as massive oversupply in the apartment market would eventually impact on the wider housing market.

Young families are now selecting smaller dwellings in their preferred locations as opposed to larger properties outside of the preferred areas.

<u>66</u> Low stock drives prices

Common wisdom suggests that spring, with its fine weather and the garden looking lush, and all that blossom, is the best season to sell. Then there's the notion that buyers starved of stock over winter will emerge in the spring and buy before the extended Christmas break is upon them.

What is often overlooked is the vast amount of stock that is held back for the spring market. Regardless of the season and the presentation, it's better to buy and sell when there's less competition, not more. There is normally an undersupply of listings in winter and an abundant supply in spring.

After Easter, as winter approaches, stock on market is usually low. Throughout 2016, for example, any buyer could have told you the lack of stock was more acute than ever. In 2013 and 2014 the Sydney and Melbourne housing markets experienced their strongest gains for those respective years during winter. In both years the prices and clearance rates eased in spring, debunking the 'sell in spring' myth.

The lack of stock on market throughout 2016 contributed to price rises unexpectedly accelerating in the Sydney and Melbourne markets. In such tight markets, it's common for every listed property to have multiple genuine bidders, reflecting its booming nature. Sellers clearly win in this equation as prices continue to hit new highs on low stock levels.

Aside from the season, another reason stock became so tight was a fear among vendors of selling and being locked out of the market. Many people looking to sell and buy in the market have a fear of selling and being unable to buy back in. There is a very real concern that house prices could continue rising after they have sold and before they have purchased, causing a self-inflicted financial loss. This concern has seen many inter-market traders hold back from listing until they have secured a home elsewhere. This phenomenon is a common but rarely mentioned side effect of a booming market.

Whether buying or selling first, it's crucial to devise a plan in advance of transacting. One of the safest ways to buy and sell in the same market is to get a delayed settlement on the first transaction. This allows time to complete the second transaction.

A lack of stock on market can create artificial strength in prices. Aim to buy, but avoid selling, at peak listing times.

<u>67</u> Buyer's agents

Is it worth employing a buyer's agent? It's a question many buyers ponder during what can be a frustrating and lengthy property search. Before deciding whether a buyer's agent can add value, be clear about what outcome you want them to achieve.

Buyer's agents promise to save you time and/or money. There is also the 'experience' factor. An experienced buyer's agent knows how the system works and can take much of the stress out of the game you need to play to secure the type of property you want. If they are well connected or networked, agents can also access good off-market listings or indicate strong interest in a certain type of property.

Time

If you provide a detailed brief of your ideal home, a buyer's agent can search for it on your behalf and save you valuable time. This aspect of their service appeals mainly to time-poor professionals, those buying remotely and buyers looking for unique, off-market opportunities.

But, like any other service, you get what you pay for, so do some market research. When employing an agent to source a property, ensure that they have excellent knowledge and a track record in the target market. Sending a buyer's agent from Unley in South Australia to find a property in the Adelaide Hills is probably not wise. As you would with any potential 'employee', check out their CV or ask for references.

If you are looking for a fairly standard property within the target market, you don't really need a buyer's agent to save you the time of sourcing suitable properties. A simple internet search will reveal a number of options.

A trap in employing agents to find you a property is that they can roll over during negotiations. They are exhausted during the search process and become anxious to 'close the deal' and move on. Just as a seller's agent can pressure the owner to drop the price to get a quick sale, the buyer's agent can pressure their buyer to pay over their preferred amount to get the job done.

Money

Once you have found the right home, you can employ a buyer's agent to handle negotiations on your behalf. By stepping back from the negotiations, you can leave the stress of the negotiation to the buyer's agent while they negotiate the best possible price.

If you employ agents solely to bid at auction or negotiate on your behalf, you are employing them for their skills rather than their time. If you judge their remuneration on time alone, it may feel like you are overpaying. But if you agree on a reward structure whereby the agent gets a higher fee if they negotiate a lower price, you are sure to get the best possible outcome. In this instance, the agent is negotiating with your money and theirs, intertwining your fortunes.

*   *   *

If their brief is simply to find a house and get a deal done, at what price and at whose cost will it be? Like a seller's agent, you want a buyer's agent to be incentivised to get the best possible result for you.

Incentivise a buyer's agent to negotiate effectively. Reward them based on the amount of money they save you.

AFTERWORD

Financial decisions tend to reflect the information on which they are based. Now you have read *Inside Real Estate*, I hope you feel better equipped with the information you need to make the right decisions when transacting real estate.

Real estate mistakes can be expensive and painful. The key to success in both rising and falling markets is to learn from the past mistakes of others. Industry spin, emotion and the salesperson's self-interest are among the main threats to the simple model of the right information = the right decision.

While writing this book I attended a national real estate conference, during which an office in Townsville was named the 'Sales Team of the Year'. Given the economic context, this was a remarkable feat by the agency.

The Townsville market had fallen year on year for the previous five years, losing 50 per cent of its value. One of the salespeople told me how he had been forced to reduce a property for which the owner had paid $340 000 to just $149 000. It was in this environment that the firm won its sales award.

The other nominees for the award were based in Melbourne and Sydney, which were enjoying a boom stretching into its fifth year. The Townsville real estate agency was achieving phenomenal success in a depressed market. The key to their success was acceptance of the market conditions, then taking the right actions to deal with this reality.

The day-to-day actions of our friends in Townsville were completely different from those of the agencies operating in the Melbourne and Sydney booms.

Consumers too can achieve success in all market conditions, if they acknowledge the current market conditions and take the required actions. *Inside Real Estate* has introduced the knowledge, strategies and actions required when buying and selling.

Generally speaking, economists have failed to understand the property market. Since 2003 they have predicted the imminent collapse of the Australian housing market. Over that time, prices have more than doubled in Sydney and Melbourne (in some instances, they have tripled). Maybe a major correction will hit the capital cities down the track, but if you had believed all the hype along the way you would have missed out on a lot of profit.

In my time in real estate, I have seen many people make and lose a lot of money in the market. The number one factor behind success in the property market is time.

Baby boomers who have owned their family home for 20 to 30 years are sitting on amazing paper profits. Those fortunate enough to have bought an investment property or three along the way have more than likely created financial independence for themselves. Negative gearing in the Australian tax system has contributed to the gains in the market for many.

At the time of writing, a client sold her investment with our agency in Balmain. When Anne purchased the property in 1990, she nearly bought a limited edition Mercedes instead. The car was almost equal in value to the cottage back then. It was only at the last minute that she went cold on buying the car and invested in the property. A quarter of a century later, the $275 000 cottage sold for well over $2 million. I don't know what became of the Mercedes.

Another success factor in the property market is the contrarian investor. This is a phenomenon that I have never been able to accept or understand. Agents are overwhelmed with buyer enquiries during a boom, but the phones are almost silent in a flat market. The cliché 'buy in gloom and sell in boom' does not seem to have caught on in real estate.

The real estate investment market is heavily driven by sentiment rather than data-based pragmatism. This phenomenon persists today. The smart money comes out in a depressed market, not at the height of a boom. Some of the best buying of the past 20 years occurred in 2008 and 2009 during the global financial crisis, as fear gripped the market.

As an occasional participant in the market, you may not have the available time to become market savvy. Reading *Inside Real Estate* should at least inspire you to source a real estate agent who is worthy of your trust.

I am happy to talk about the digital threat to real estate agents because I know the good agents aren't threatened at all. There has always been and always will be a place for professional real estate agents.

Consumers tend to go through three phases in their relations with estate agents. They detest them, then they accept them and finally they embrace them. It is only when you positively need an estate agent that you begin to distinguish and appreciate the true professionals among the herd.

As much as I respect professional real estate agents, I cringe at the pedestal on which agents and other 'wealth managers' are placed in our society. Many others carry out nobler work in the community for much lower pay and less kudos. These hard-working members of society often consolidate their work and wealth in real estate, which brings us back to the important role played by agents.

While agents are not the source of their clients' wealth, they often help negotiate it. There is absolutely no doubt that the barrier to entry into a real estate sales career should be raised. The stakes are often high yet the experience of many agents is shockingly limited. The regulation and training of agents should also be increased.

Until these things happen, it is up to the individual consumer—you—to control your own destiny.

Thank you for taking the time to read *Inside Real Estate*. I welcome your comments or feedback: you can contact me at peter@harrispartners.com.au.

INDEX